JOURNEY
INTO
JAINISM

A collection of short stories

By
Samani Smit Pragya
(Sadhvi Vishruta Vibha)

An imprint of
B. Jain Publishers (P) Ltd.
USA — EUROPE — INDIA

Price: Rs. 75.00

JOURNEY INTO JAINISH

First Edition: 1996
4th Impression: 2012

All rights reserved. No part of this book may be reproduced, stored in a retrie system or transmitted, in any form or by any means, mechanical, photocopy recording or otherwise, without any prior written permission of the publisher.

© with the publisher

Published by Kuldeep Jain for

HEALTH HARMONY

An imprint of
B. JAIN PUBLISHERS (P) LTD.
1921/10, Chuna Mandi, Paharganj, New Delhi 110 055 (INDIA)
Tel.: +91-11-4567 1000   Fax: +91-11-4567 1010
Email: info@bjain.com   Website: **www.bjain.com**

Printed in India by
J.J. Offset Printers

ISBN: 978-81-319-9914-1

BLESSING

If there were no stories to tell man would be deprived of the fragrance of life which is the essence of it. The beauty of the flower is in its fragrance. It does not need any definition. How can one define "story"? That which assimilates with life in its own nature.

Having accepted this natural aspect, both the traditions--1. Loukik (worldly) 2. Aloukik (beyond) have given it due importance and valuation. No literature of any tradition is devoid of stories. Jain literature is divided into four parts. One of them is stories. Original scriptures as well as the subsequent works are all rich in interesting stories. Samani Smit Pragya (initiated in the order as Sadhvi Vishrut Vibha on 18th Oct. '92) while travelling on her various assignments abroad has been approached by people living there with a request to write a few interesting stories in English for the young generation. That very demand turned into her inspiration. After some successful dives into the deep ocean of Jain literature, she came out with a few rare pearls.

The necessity of having Jain literature in English is felt not only in foreign countries but in India as well where the new generation is being educated through the English medium. This book will probably serve their purpose. A lot more may be expected from Sadhvi Vishrut Vibha who will incessantly be active in this field.

10/4/94　　　　　　　　　　　　　　Acharya Mahaprajna
Jaipur

PROLOGUE

Story is a very impressive way of presenting literature which is most attractive to kids, youths, as well as the older generation. Its special purpose is that it approaches the reader's mind and heart with utter simplicity. Even the most difficult and serious subjects may be conveyed through this media with ease. We have a treasure of interesting as well as inspiring stories in Jain Agamas (scriptures).

Acharya Shri Tulsi wants the people settled abroad and specially the young generation to have a soild base of Jain culture and philosophy.

Sadhvi Vishrut Vibha, disciple of Acharya Shri Tulsi, has written some selected historical and canonical stories in English. "Journey into Jainism" is her first attempt. I trust, Jains and others interested living abroad as well as in India should be able to grasp the doctrines of Jainism through this book and thereby encourage the authoress to proceed further in her attempt with greater enthusiasm.

Sadhvi Pramukha Kanak Prabha

11/4/94
Jaipur

PREFACE

Man is constantly engaged to gain material prosperity and in the process has lost touch with himself. Only a few people pay attention towards upliftment of human and spiritual values. Acharya Shri Tulsi is one of them. He is a great Acharya of Jain religion. He always thinks about the moral and spiritual development of the masses. This is why he sponsored Anuvrat movement for cultivating moral values. He also started "Preksha Meditation" in order to relieve mental, physical and emotional tensions, and "Science of living" for developing an integrative personality.

Moreover, he is very conscious about Jainism. Though monks and nuns are making incessant efforts to propagate Jain religion but due to their rigid code of conduct, they are bound to travel on foot only. Therefore, Acharya Shri Tulsi felt a need to start a new order called "Saman Order" who could travel abroad. This order was started in 1980 at Ladnun in Rajasthan.

I was one of the first few to get the golden opportunity to be initiated in this group. I spent my twelve years in the Saman Order. Not only did I study Jain canonical literature but also undertook journies abroad in order to spread the message of Lord Mahavir. With this mission I went to many parts of Europe, America, Canada, Hong Kong, Thailand, etc. When I was in London and America I found that children took great interest in the Jain historical stories. I used to tell them lots of stories and they suggested to me to put them down in a book form. At that very time I decided to write the stories. I thought that stories are a good media to make them understand our history, culture and the principles of Jainism.

I would like to thank Miss Sunita (D/o Mool Chand Singhi) who lives in New Jersey (America). She read the stories carefully, asked many questions about them and took up the praiseworthy task of editing them. Special thanks to Mahendra Muni who went through the stories and made them authentic from the historical point of view.

Finally, I am very grateful to Gurudeva Shri Tulsi, Acharya Shri Mahaprajna and Sadhvi Pramukha Kanak Prabhaji who are the very source of my enthusiasm in every walk of life. I pray Acharya Shri and Yuvacharya Shri may bestow their blessings so that I may further improve in my endeavours.

Sadhvi Vishrut Vibha

11/4/94
Jaipur

Table of Contents

The Value of Equanimity 3
The Value of Non-Violence 6
The value of Pure Thought (1) 10
The Value of Pure Thought (2) 13
The Value of Resolution 16
The Value of Forgiveners 22
The Value of Self-Control 27
The Value of Simple-Heartedness 35
The Value of Contentment 37
The Value of Inspiration 39
The Value of Renunciation (1) 43
The Value of Renunciation (2) 49
The Value of Tolerance (1) 55
The Value of Tolerance (2) 58
The Value of Satisfaction 63
The Value of Forbearance 65
The Value of Giving Alms 68
The Value of Humbleness 71
The Value of Self-Realization 74
The Value of Repentance (1) 76

The Value of Repentance (2)	79
The Value of Truthfulness	81
The Value of Kindness	83
The Value of Calmness	90
The Value of Controlling Greed	92
The Value of Self-Analysis	94
The Value of Modesty	98
The Value of Purity	101
The Value of Celibacy	105
The Value of Chastity	110
The Value of Faith	115
The Value of Detachment	118
The Value of Patience	121
The Value of Monkhood	126
The Value of Self-Awareness	129
Glossary of Terms	131

The Value of Equanimity

Prince Lalitangkumar was the son of King Kumbha, the ruler of Amarpur. He was very handsome and was loved by all the members of his family.

Once Acharya Dharmaghosa came to the city. The prince, listening to the acharya's sermon, was very much influenced and impressed by it. After receiving permission from his parents, he became a monk.

He was given the name 'Kuurgaduk' because he loved to eat the coarse grain known as *'Kuur.'* As a monk, he wanted to learn to control his sensory organs. However, as he could not bear the pangs of hunger, he did not observe fast and would instead eat *kuur.*

On the starting day of the *Chaturmaas,* all the monks including the Acharya as well as all the lay-followers observed fast. Because the Acharya inspired all his followers to do penance, some of them fasted for one, two, or even four months. During the time of fast, Acharya was busy with his lectures.

It was excruciatingly difficult for Kuurgaduk *muni* to remain without food. He was waiting for the lecture to conclude so that he might collect alms and eat his *kuur.* Because of his immense appetite he could not desist from satisfying his hunger. Thus he went to Acharya after the sermon to seek permission to collect alms. Acharya was once again disappointed, "All are fasting; you should do it too."

Muni Kuurgaduk replied, "I know you are saying this for my benefit and welfare. I know the value and usefulness of fasting, but I regret I am unable to do it. Please exempt me from fasting and allow me to eat *kuur.*" The Acharya, exasperated, at last gave his consent the *muni* to gather the alms.

It was excruciatingly difficult for Kuurgaduk muni to remain without food. He was waiting for the lecture to conclude so that he might collect alms and eat his kurr.

In spite of the half-hearted approval by the Acharya, the *muni* went out in search of food. When he obtained some, he brought it back to show the Acharya, who, upon seeing it, lost his temper and rebuked him. He spat on the food. Kuurgaduk remained completely equanimous.

Kuurgaduk went into his room and sat down with his food, slowly seeing the Acharya's point of view. He thought it over with complete equanimity of mind. While eating his food, his mind was absorbed in meditation and re-evaluation of his habit. Then he stopped eating; he had experienced a state of purity of thought and then the climax of forgiveness.

Meanwhile, a goddess named Chakreshvari appeared and asked the monks, "Where is Kuurgaduk muni?" They told her first to visit the Acharya and asked her, "Why are you so eager to see Kuurgaduk who is attached to food?" Whereupon the goddess replied, "I have come here to visit only him. Simandhardswami, the Omniscient *Tirthankara,* told me that *muni* Kuurgaduk has attained omniscience."

All the *munis* ridiculed her at this, nevertheless pointed to the place where the *muni* was sitting. She went there and did *vandanaa* to him. He was absorbed in meditation and had indeed attained *kevalgyaana.* Many gods celebrated the *kaivalya* function of the monk. His *acharya,* however, was surprised to learn of it. Then, he too repented for his anger and attained enlightenment.

The Value of Non-Violence

After the demise of notorious butcher Kaalasaukarik of Rajgriha, there was to be a celebration of his son Sulas's ascension to the post of 'the head of the family'. The family wished to conduct it in the traditional manner, with great pomp and show. Therefore, a buffalo was ordered and Sulas was handed a shining sword and asked to slay it with one stroke.

Sulas was terrified. He had never imagined that such an abominable task would be allotted to him to perform. Yet, he was a butcher by family tradition-- his father could kill five hundred buffaloes a day. Under no condition or temptation would his father give up his daily routine. Even a royal punishment could not alter his tendency for killing.

Once, Shrenik, the king of Magadha, forbade the killing of buffaloes for one day. Kaalsaukarrik's disobedience of the order enraged the king, who then forced him to descend into a deep pit (a dry well). Kaalsaukarik, who regarded the killing of buffaloes as a duty in conformity with his family tradition, was perplexed at this attempt to annihilate it.

After a deep reflection over the problem, Kaalsaukarik at last found an outlet for the raging fire of violence that was burning in him. He collected the mud in the well and shaped it into buffaloes and thus fulfilled his duty by killing those buffaloes.

Sulas was disheartened at this violent tendency of his father, but any attempt to change his father's behavioral pattern was futile. Yet, even with such violence around him, Sulas retained a calm, peaceful, non-violent attitude. Although sad about his father's death, Sulas was internally delighted that henceforth his house would be completely free from cruelty.

When the sword was given to him to perform the rites, he began to tremble. The buffalo standing before him looked as if praying to Sulas to spare its life. Sulas deciphered the silent language of the helpless animal and felt its pain within himself. With a deep groan, the boy expressed his unwillingness and helplessness to kill it.

This was a great shock to the family brought up in superstitions and strict conventions. His family was unhappy at this intransigence of Sulas. They did't know what to do. On one hand there was the firm, noble, non-violent determination of Sulas, and on the other hand there was the brutal family tradition.

Some time passed whilst Sulas was as adamant as ever. The family searched their petty brains for an answer. At last it was decided that Sulas should inflict the first blow on the buffalo simply to observe the tradition and the remaining formalities would be taken up by other people.

Sulas now stiffened his trembling hands. He tightened his grip upon the sword, mustered all the strength he could, and swung the weapon without further deliberation. The blow, was not on the buffalo, but on his own legs. As the blood gushed forth like an angry stream, the members of his family were filled with great surprise, fear and perplexity.

The blow was not on the buffalo, but on his own legs.

Getting his chance to speak on the matter at last, Sulas exclaimed, "Fellow creatures of the earth! I have a word for you ! Please listen to me ! Even as we like to protect our lives, this buffalo seeks to save his. We care about ourselves but not about those other creatures who have as much right to live as we ourselves have! This I cannot understand. Why do we not treat them with the respect they deserve ? If our positions were reversed, we would not stand to be treated thus!"

For our own spiritual good, we must realize the relative equality among all living beings and must not treat any as inferior, because they do, after all, love as we do, suffer as we do, and have likes and dislikes as we do. Our actions must be the product of knowledge, not ignorance! We must exercise self-control and, in the true Jain way, not kill or hurt any creature through our action, speech, or thought.

The Value of Pure Thought (1)

King Prasannachandra ruled over the small state of Pottanpur. At last came the time for him to transfer his royal authority to his son, who had just come of age. After entrusting the management of the State to his son, Prasannachandra received initiation from Lord Mahavir.

Once Prasannachandra, now a monk, came to Rajgriha with Lord Mahavir. Standing on one leg, with arms raised, he was engrossed in meditation outside the *Samavasaran*. A large number of people, including King Shrenik, passed by without disturbing the deep meditation of the monk to see Mahavir.

Seeing the calm, quiet face of Prasannachandra, resplendent in meditational pose, Durmukh, a minister of King Shrenik, was possessed by a fit of mad jealousy and malicious intent to disturb the monk's tranquillity. He taunted, "Having left your son, a minor, at the helm of affairs of your kingdom, you have become a carefree monk. Do you know how fearful your young son is in such a situation? Enemies have surrounded him on all sides! The kingdom and his life both are at stake! If you have any worth, show it. It is your duty to save your child from these perils, after which you should think of spiritual attainments."

Outwardly, Prasannachandra was unperturbed, but inwardly, his mind was growing restless. He visualized the frightened face of his young, helpless child and he was mentally there at Pottanpur to protect his son. Mentally, he ordered the army to be prepared for battle, saw his army carry out the order, and even come with arms onto the battlefield, wounded or imprisoned all who threatened to harm the well-being of his son.

His thoughts now directed to their proper sphere, Prasannachandra had pure thoughts and new vision.

This agonizing state of mind full of violence and fear were contradictory to the peaceful outward nature that he was manifesting. New thoughts were perpetually fueling the fire of wrath and vengeance burning within his mind. Upon hearing the appreciative words of a humble layman thanking him for his exemplary lifestyle-- "Leaving all worldly luxuries and practising *Sadhana* is noble indeed"--

the monk began to really think: -- Whose son? Whose empire? Of what am I thinking? Why do these earthly cares plague me so? What good can come of wishing harm for others? Such attachment is not wise. I must repudiate such inane feelings as victory and defeat. Such are the thoughts of irrational men. I wish to be beyond such trifles.

His thoughts now directed to their proper sphere, Prasannachandra had pure thoughts and new vision. The mental enemies disappeared; the delusion was over. The veils so long obscuring knowledge and perception were flung aside, thus clearing his path of all obstructions. Prasannachandra had attained omniscience.

The Value of Pure Thought (2)

Marudevaa was the mother of Rishabha, the first *Tirthankar* (prophet) in Jain religion. She was a very benevolent and pure-hearted lady. Because she was beyond the wasteful emotions of anger, pride, deceit and greed, the bondage of her *karma* was not intense. After Rishabha's initiation into the monkhood, she lost interest in housework, and instead spent her time on religious performances.

For a long period of time following Rishabha's initiation, Marudevaa could not visit him. One day, after attaining supreme knowledge, Lord Rishabha came back to Ayodhya.

For some time his mother had been worried about him. She pondered over what would happen to Rishabha after he renounced the world, who would serve him, who would take care of him! At times, because of her strong bonds of attachment to Rishabha, she thought, "Rishabha should have kept me in mind, because, after all, I am his mother." When she thought of Rishabha, she was choked with emotion. When she learned of Rishabha's arrival, she was overjoyed. Jubilantly she made preparations to visit Rishabha and to make up for the lost time between them.

The festivities commenced. As she sat high on an elephant, a flow of thoughts passed forth in her mind.

When she looked at Rishabha in the rostrum from afar, her previous thoughts changed. She thought, 'Rishabha lives in great contentment. I was unnecessarily worried about him. A great number of human and celestial beings are serving him. He did not have such prosperity as a householder.'

Thus, her thoughts became pure and she too achieved the state of Kevalgyana.

As these petty thoughts ran through her head, she began to reprimand herself, 'Where am I going? What am I thinking? Rishabha has attained supreme knowledge and yet I have delusion in my mind. He has become detached and I am still attached. This is not good for me.'

The Value of Pure Thought (2)

Thus, her thoughts became pure and she too achieved the state of *Kevalgyana*. Lord Rishabha, who was giving his lecture, told that Marudevaa had been liberated. All looked behind and found that only the physical body of Marudevaa remained.

According to Jain doctrine, purity of thought guides a person on the path to spiritual upliftment.

The Value of Resolution

Bhaavadeva and Bhavadeva were two brothers. Their mother, Revati, was a deeply religious lady who was very firm in her observance of daily rituals. The religious nature of the mother left an indelible impression on Bhavadeva. He also became religious and condemnatory of sin.

During adolescence, his religious tendency augmented immensely. The increase in his detachment towards worldly things eventually resulted in his becoming a monk. His brother, Bhaavadeva, as a householder, continued to perform religious duties in his mother's company.

As Bhaavadeva came of age, he was wedded to a beautiful girl named Naagala. Bhaavadeva was returning home with his bride when he saw his elder brother giving a sermon in the forest. Realizing this as a chance to open his brother's eyes, *muni* Bhavadeva highlighted the transitoriness and shelterlessness of the world. The preachings took their toll of Bhaavadeva. Listening to them he desired to leave the carnal pleasures to enjoy the wholesome simplicity of the life of a monk.

However, Bhaavadeva's coin was two-sided, and he could not tell which side was up. He told his brother, "When I look at you, I want to join the assembly of monks and nuns; yet when I look at my wife, I want to fulfil my duty towards her."

The Value of Resolution

Realising this as a chance to open his brother's eyes muni Bhaavadeva highlighted the transitoriness and shelterlessness of world.

Naagala then spoke, soothing her husband, "Do not worry about me. If you desire to adopt the religious path, you may. I cannot take to this difficult path but will not prove an obstacle for you. I shall pass my life with my religious mother-in-law. So many indulge in carnal desires that those persons who abstain from them are truly special. They are not the common people but are great souls. Please, if you feel strongly about it, accept the path which you feel so right, without further ado."

The encouragement of his brother, the inspiration of his wife and his own innate inclination toward the monkhood, all effected Bhaavadeva's initiation into the life of penance and seclusion. Naagala remained accordingly with her pious mother-in-law.

Days, months and years rolled on. Bhavadeva and Bhaavadeva busied themselves in meditation and penance. They rambled from town to town to deliver their sermons to awaken the people. Now, as Bhavadeva muni grew old, Bhaavadeva, still in the prime of his life, quite often changed his mind.

For instance, he would think, "What a fool I was to get involved in this affair! I am not certain that this way of sadhana, remaining hungry, wandering from place to place, is entirely the right way to achieve the desired end." Then he would counteract this by thinking, "I am on this path of my own accord. I should walk the path I choose and do my utmost to fulfil my expectations." In weighing the pros and cons of his situation in life, the attraction toward monkhood diminished and the allurement for worldly objects became ever eminent. He again wanted to be a householder and husband. But then he thought, "My elder brother and his old age! I should not leave him thus!" Though still a monk, Bhaavadeva was now inclined toward the household. He consoled himself that, "When Bhavadeva muni breathes his last I can change my course as I see fit."

Bhavadeva muni, wrinkled from old age and penance, adopted santhaara, and faced death like a brave one. Bhaavadeva was now unbridled, as no one could now prevent him from following the wrong path. Happily he proceeded toward his village, entertaining felicitous ideas in his mind along the way. Then, however, darker thoughts began clouding his brain, "If my mother is alive, she will not allow me to live with my family that I had

The Value of Resolution

renounced," after which he assured himself that, "if Bhavadeva muni had died, the mother must also have died."

Thus thinking he reached the outskirts of the village in the guise of muni. Naagala was one of a group of women passing by. Seeing the monk, she approached and bowed to him. Bhaavadeva asked her, "Do you live in this village?" When she replied in the affirmative, he asked, "Do you know the famous householder Revati ?"

Naagala answered, "We all knew her, for she was a religious lady in our town," after which Bhaavadeva continued, "Is she happy these days?" He at last received the massage which he had sought, "She died many years ago." Bhaavadeva felt it a boon, 'Now there is no obstacle blocking my way to my cherished object.' He further inquired, "Do you know her daughter-in-law ? Where does she live? How is she doing these days?"

Naagala now recognized her husband, but could not fathom why he had come and why he was asking her such questions. She did not reveal her identity, but rather tried to elicit from him some comprehensible information.

Naagala: I know her very well. She is also a religious lady like her mother-in-law. She has adopted the life of celibacy forever, and inspired her husband to do the same.. Why are you asking me such questions about women ? It does not behove a monk.

Bhaavadeva: Naagala is my wife and that is why I am enquiring about her.

Naagala: A Jain monk has no wife. What are you saying?

Bhaavadeva: True, a monk has no wife, but I had accepted initiation just after my marriage. At that time I met muni Bhavadeva in the forest and thought it to be the right path for me, and yet now.....

Naagala: O monk! As a friend of Naagala, I tell you frankly that she will not now like to live with you. Do not now astray from your path.

Bhaavadeva: How can you say that about her? If I am so fond of her, I think she too should be so fond of me. She might have been waiting for me a long time. She is a true devotee of her husband, and so would certainly wish me home.

Naagala: Tell me one thing, O monk! Where would you stay? Please dwell upon the problems herein while I go and find Naagala.

Bhaavadeva was ruminating on his future plans, on his household relationship with Naagala, when, all of a sudden, a child came running toward his mother, and the following conversation ensued:

Son : O mother! I thank you for the table of such sweet dishes as you did lay before me! I had not known such great delight before.

Mother: I am glad, my son.

Son: But mother! As I was finishing my *kheer*, there appeared a fly in the dish. I vomited, and then licked that vomit. I did not waste it.

Mother: Thank you, son! I am proud of you ! I am sure that in the future you will again act with such frugality.

The Value of Resolution

Bhaavadeva, listening to this conversation, grew bewildered and repulsed. Indignantly he exclaimed, "How degraded you are! Who would eat vomit like that! Your son ate it and you appreciate it in such a way."

Hearing this rebuke by Bhaavadeva, Naagala roared like a lioness: "Monk! This child ate vomit, but he was ignorant. Think about yourself! Are you any better? You left the worldly pleasures and carnal desires which were like this vomit that so excites your disgust, and yet now you want to eat the same vomit! You have read Agamas, undertaken austerities and hard way of life, and now you are giving up your attainments. You should look before you leap! The serpent leaves his upper skin and never turns back to see it. Look at me. You are behaving like a mad person for Naagala who is standing before you.

"I want to make this point clear: I will not indulge in worldly love. I can respect you as a monk, but I cannot accept you as my husband. You are ready to break your vow but I am firm. No attraction can change my ideas. It would be better for you to go to the forest and perform penance. I hope that you will attain the same path which your elder brother had adopted."

The words of Naagala sparked something within him. He was suddenly awakened. He felt as if he had been given a light to see through the darkness. He thanked Naagala, left the town and returned to the forest to accomplish his sadhana and attain the desired goal.

The Value of Forgiveness

Dridhaprahaari was born in a wealthy Brahman family. Although his father was an honest and religious person, Dridhaprahaari was addicted to all the seven vices, including drinking, meat-eating, stealing and gambling. His father, a worthy man, tried unsuccessfully to persuade his son to give up his immoral habits, but Dridhaprahaari made no attempt to correct his deplorable behavior. His father, finally overcome with antipathy, threw his disgraceful son out of the house. In doing so, though, he incurred the wrath of his son, who then set off and joined a thieves' gang. He became a practised highway robber, plundering and killing many innocent people.

Generally impressed by his malignancy and ruffianism, the leader of this gang was extremely pleased with Dridhaprahaari, and thought him very dexterous. In view of his unbending courage and his matchless and unfailing style of inflicting a blow, the aged chief dubbed him "Dridhaprahaari" (one who hits hard), and regarded him as his own son. Soon Dridhaprahaari was held in high esteem by the whole gang, and finally he became the chief of the gang. All the thieves now worked under his instructions.

Accompanied by his comrades-in-arms, he looted a great town and collected enormous amount of booty, killing many people. After a while, Dridhaprahaari took rest in the home of a Brahman. There was the Brahman, his wife and their children in the house. His children were anxious to eat the *kheer* their mother was preparing.

Dridhaprahaari was also invited to have lunch there. As the smell of food reached his nostrils, however, he could not control himself and came to the kitchen uncalled by the lady of the house. As he sat down beside the pot of kheer, the Brahman's wife became upset. Scolding him she said, "O fool! You should know the fact that after your touching this sweet preparation,, it will be of no avail to us. Therefore, please sit at some distance. I shall offer you food later on. You should observe the traditions of this household, because the house of a Brahmin does not allow its food to be touched by anybody else until offered."

Dridhaprahaari was extremely angered by the rebuke. He could not control his emotions and cut the Brahman's wife with his sword into two pieces on the spot. Hearing the horrible screams, the Brahman, who was in the bathroom, rushed to the scene to help. Dridhaprahaari killed him too. A cow who was nearby witnessed the gruesome murder in the family and came running to take revenge. As Dridhaprahaari's blow was always unfailing, he gave such a blow with his sword that the cow's stomach was cut in two pieces. The cow had been at the advanced stage of pregnancy. The embryo, writhing in pain, came out. It was a very pitiable and heart-rending sight. On one side there were Brahman and his wife, on the other side there were the cow and the calf coming out prematurely from the womb. Violence was at its apex. If the heart of a person does not melt at such a scene, really it is not heart, it is stone.

Dridhaprahaari, standing in the midst of such pathos, could not help but be affected by it. He was, after all, a human being and possessed some sensitivity. Compassion was now awakened in his heart. This flow of compassion was so immense that he felt pity and regret for what he had done. Now was a time of significant reflection and introspection for Dridhaprahaari.

The recalled all the disgusting incidents in his past and present life. He was replete with self -- condemnation. The dormant feeling of humanity agitated his soul, and he thought, "I am a human being. I feel pleasure and pain. Does it behove of me as a human being to snatch others' lives, steal money and torture them? Even an animal like a cow can sacrifice its life to relieve the sufferings of its master. Furthermore, it has some discretion. My heart is never moved by such horrible deeds. What can possibly be more cruel and inhuman than this? Dridhaprahaari, thoroughly repulsed with himself and seeking to purify his soul, discarded his sword and clothes and left the house in changed robes.

Thus did the tyrant thief now adopt monkhood, uproot his hair and give up his household life. He thought to himself, "I will go to the wild forests, perform penance, sit in meditational posture and pass on into deep ecstasy. I shall restrain the bodily movements. I have hurt the feelings of thousands of people. I have killed a number of infants. I have made many young ladies widows. I have troubled thousands of people by purloining property worth

The Value of Forgiveness

millions of rupees. They must all desire retaliation against me. I must do *Kaayotsarg* out of the town. There I will have to bear more sufferings, which shall be conducive to the shedding off of the *karmas.*"

Dridhaprahaari stood in the posture of relaxation on the eastern gate of the town. Hundreds of men, women and children passed by that way. As he did, many became upset and enraged, saying, "You have killed my father," or "You have killed my uncle and wife." Some threw sand at his eyes and still others pelted stones at him. Muni Dridhaprahaari remained very calm, and remained deeply engrossed in *kaayotsarg* for one and a half month. He forgave all. Gradually, people became less hostile, as they realized that Dridhaprahaari was sorry for what he had done and was sincerely trying to make amends.

Hundreds of men, women and children passed by that way. As he did, many became upset and enraged, saying, "you have killed my father", or "You have killed my uncle and wife."

Dridhaprahaari departed from that place and started *kaayotsarg* at the next gate of the town. There also did the people scold him, but he pocketed all the insults. He bore all tortures with complete forgiveness and accomplished *kaayotsarg*. As he was adept in theft, in the same way he was resolute and steadfast in religion. He put into practice Lord Mahavira's saying, "The brave in physical action are also brave in religious affairs." After severe penance for six months, he obtained *kevalgyaana*.

The Value of Self-Control

Having been initiated as a *muni,* Sthuulibhadra was completely engrossed in the religious study of scriptures as well as spiritual practice. On account of his sharp intellect, he became well conversant with the Agmas.

On the eve of the start of *Chaturmaas,* four monks came to their Guru. The first of these monks announced, "Renouncing all food and water, I want to go into deep meditation for these four months in the cave of a great lion."

The second one declared, " I want to be absorbed in deep *kaayotsarg* in a place where poisonous snakes live."

The third one proclaimed to the guru, "I intend to meditate uninterruptedly at a river-bank from where maidens take water."

The fourth one, Muni Sthuulibhadra, expressed his desire, "I wish to pass this rainy retreat at the Art Gallery of Kosha, a famous prostitute. It was where I had spent my past twelve years. Now I shall perform a particular penance there."

Judging their capabilities, the Guru allowed them to do as they had planned. The first three monks reached their respective destinations and became absorbed in meditation, penance and study.

Muni Sthuulibhadra arrived at the residence of Kosha in Patliputra. As she watched him coming to her home, she immediately forgot any past disappointments and sorrow. When Muni Sthuulibhadra said, "I want to spend my *Chaturmaas* in your art gallery," Kosha was ecstatic. She exclaimed, "O holy sir! How lucky I am! Please treat this art gallery as your own. I am also for you. There is no need to seek permission from anyone else. I have been waiting for you."

When muni Sthuulibhadra said "I want to spend my chaturmass in your art gallery", Kosha was ecstatic. She explained, 'O holy Sir! How lucky I am! Please treat this art gallery as your own. I am also for you.

The *Chaaturmaas* began. Muni Sthuulibhadra engaged himself wholeheartedly in the deep study of scriptures and meditation. Occasionally, Kosha would express her feelings to him and remind him of their previous love for each other. Muni Sthuulibhadra heard her reminiscences, but never commented.

When all her efforts failed to bear fruit, and she lost all hopes of winning him over, Muni Sthuulibhadra spoke some soothing words, "Kosha, there was a time when we were attached excessively in the bond of love. At that stage, the whole universe seemed insignificant except us. We thought we were in pure ecstasy, but in reality it was just illusion. True happiness cannot be achieved through any person, substance, or circumstance. It is absolute and is the true nature of the soul. Before, I was attracted to you, but since my father's demise, I have obtained a greater understanding. Now I am able to dive deep into reality and to experience a true and indescribable joy. I have pure feelings towards you; you seem to me to be my sister, and you should also view me as your brother."

These beautiful words from a spiritual practitioner melted the heart of Kosha. Detachment took shape instead of sexual instincts. Muni Sthuulibhadra gave his lecture for four months, and changed the heart of Kosha. He had come there with the moral purpose of giving her true knowledge and of revealing the path to a virtuous, meaningful life. In this attempt he had succeeded. Kosha was thereafter a religious householder, a follower of the twelve vows enjoined upon a laywoman.

At the end of *Chaaturmaas,* all the monks except Sthuulibhadra came before the Guru, who gave them due regard and praised them for performing their severe penance successfully. At last, Muni Sthuulibhadra arrived and bowed down at the lotus feet of his Guru. All were looking at him, waiting to see what the Guru would say to him who had not undergone any penance during his *chaaturmaas*.

The Guru received him warmly, "Oh, welcome! you have performed the most difficult job." The other monks were astonished to hear these words. The monk who had spent his *Chaaturmaas* in the cave of a lion thought to himself, "We three monks, who did severe penance at the risk of our lives, were blessed with only the expression 'difficult task'. While he who enjoyed the pleasures of the prostitute's house for four months has been addressed as the doer of the 'most difficult task. It shows that the Guru is prejudiced. Because Sthuulibhadra is the son of the minister, a special favour is shown towards him. Well, if I too pass the next *Chaaturmaas* there, will our guru think as highly of me?"

As the time of the next *Chaaturmaas* came near, and the monks again made their requests, the monk who had passed the former *Chaaturmaas* in the lion's cave now asked to be allowed to spend the four months at the house of Kosha. The wise Guru immediately comprehended the situation, and politely explained to the monk, "It is an extremely difficult task. Please believe me when I say that you cannot do justice to it. You cannot do any penance with feelings of jealousy. Remember that we are leading lives of *sadhaks*."

The muni, however, lost his temper and exclaimed, "Nothing is too difficult for me. I have decided to go there and am resolute in my decision." The guru tried to discourage him further, "It is not suitable for you. If you

The Value of Self-Control

go there, you will deviate from your accumulated virtues. You will not succeed in your attempt."

Neglecting the Guru's advice, the muni left for his destination, at last reaching the house of Kosha. Kosha perceived the hidden meaning of the monk's arrival. Now that she was a religious householder, she felt it her duty not to let the monk deviate from his path.

As the *Chaaturmaas* progressed, the *muni* lived too comfortable a life, enjoying such pleasures and luxuries as tasty meals and idleness. Furthermore, as the beauty of Kosha was ever in front of him, he gave up all religious activities, and put forth a proposal before her. The conversation went as follows:

Kosha - *Muni!* You know that we covet money. Therefore, tell me what you possess.

Muni - How can we have money? We are but monks.

Kosha - Well, we follow a rule of excessive attachment to wealth. If we do not, how can we lead our lives?

Muni - Is there any way out of it?

Kosha - (after some thought)- There is one way, but that depends only on your succeeding in it. It might prove to be a difficult job.

Muni - What is it? I do not regard any task too difficult for the sake of you.

Kosha - Well, the king of Nepal gives away a jewel rug worth one and a quarter lakh rupees. If you could bring it, your desire shall be fulfilled.

Thus, mad in his love for Kosha, the *muni* completely forgot the code of conduct befitting monkhood and left for Nepal in a state of obsession. After confronting a great many hardships, the monk finally arrived before the king, who then gave him the jewel rug. As he began leaving Nepal, however, the people advised him to conceal it so that robbers might not steal it. Now he cautiously hid the rug in the hollow of a bamboo stick which he carried on his shoulder, and continued on his way.

On his way to Kosha's house, a parrot uttered the words, "One lakh rupees are being brought through this path." As a result, some thieves came out of hiding and approached the monk. When they could not find anything, and the monk pleaded, "I have no precious thing," they at last released him.

As he continued his journey towards Patliputra, however, the parrot again cried about the one lakh rupees. This cry brought forth the chief of the thieves, who accosted and searched the *muni*. The monk again replied that he had nothing with him. To this, the chief said that the parrot had never told a lie. After receiving severe rebuke from this chief, Muni finally became helpless and narrated the whole episode to the chief, and prayed for the rug for himself. The chief, feeling compassion for the poor monk, did not snatch the jewel rug after all.

The *muni* proceeded on his journey and eventually reached the house of Kosha. The pleased monk eagerly told her, "I have brought the jewel rug for you. Now you should accept my proposal." At this, Kosha replied, "I am ready for you, but first, I shall take my bath."

The Value of Self-Control

The, *muni* waited for her. As Kosha emerged from the bathroom, she wiped her feet on the expensive rug, and then dropped it into a dirty drain. For this, she was reprimanded by the monk, who angrily exclaimed, "You seem to be an idiot. You don't know how much I had to go through to procure it. How could you throw it in such filth?"

Kosha exhibited a look of surprise and inquired, "What is the matter?" Muni indignantly declared, "You do not perceive the importance of this rug and the hard efforts I have made to obtain it. Do you not know the value of it? You cannot get such rugs in your lifetime. You should have handled it very carefully."

Kosha, now feeling extremely sad, told the *muni,* "You should ponder deeply over this incident. What are you doing? You are worried about the rug, but not about your own soul. You see the hill burning but you cannot see what is going on under your sole."

The *muni* had forgotten his aim in life completely. He could not understand the meaning of Kosha's words. He was concerned only about the beauty of Kosha. He impatiently asked, "What are you talking about? Did you forget my proposal?"

Kosha replied scoldingly, "I did not forget your proposal. Forget me for one minute and look into your heart. You were born in a noble family. With the feeling of great detachment, you have renounced your property and family. You have done much penance. Why are you now getting enamored of me? When you accepted the noble path, had you any exception for me? Muni, you have paid much attention to this rug, but you have forgotten your own soul."

She further said, "You claim you love me, but don't you believe that the carnal desires of yours are totally responsible for causing all the troubles you have undergone. You are leaving your *sadhana* in exchange for the flesh. Out of sheer foolishness, you have forgotten your vows. You envied Sthuulibhadra, but you are no match for him. We loved each other for twelve years, and when he was back in my life again, I was restless for him. Yet he did not deviate from his path. He did not bend before me but made me an ideal woman. When you came here, you were firm on your ideals, and I was the same in my vows. Yet you slipped from the right, moral path. Do you believe it to be good? Do you realize the value of human life?"

Hearing this sharp rebuke, realization dawned on the monk. He was ashamed of himself and was filled with self-condemnation.

Again did Kosha speak, "Even now, the time has not passed. You have not fully strayed from your path. It is time for you to go to your guru, take the repentance, and achieve purity once more. He will show you the right path. Also, forgive me for the trouble I have caused you, but it was only to make you perfect in your *sadhana.*

Immensely inspired by Kosha's words, Muni went to the guru, took repentance, and became pure.

The Value of Simple-Heartedness

One day, Atimuktaka, the son of King Vijay in Pollaspur, was playing with his friends when he saw Gautama Swami, who was the chief disciple and an apostle of Lord Mahavir, passing that way.

"Who are you? Where are you going?" Atimuktaka asked him.

"I am a Jain monk and am going to collect my alms," replied Gautama Swami.

"Can you take food from my home too?" asked Atimuktaka.

"Why not?" replied Gautama Swami.

Atimuktaka brought him to his home holding him by the hand. After taking his food, Gautam Swami returned with Atimuktaka.

Atimuktaka listened attentively to Gautama Swami's lecture about Mahavir Swami and, enchanted by it, instantly and eagerly became ready to leave his household life at once. At first his parents were very reluctant to allow him for his initiation but finally they had to agree. He then became a monk.

One day, while he was out in the forest looking at the river he forgot about his monkhood. He put his begging bowl on the flowing water. He was very elated by it and began to scream joyfully, "My bowl is floating in the river, fast moving on to the other bank, so am I, striving for spiritual mirth, crossing the barrier of death and birth."

My bowl is floating in the river, fast moving on to the other bank, so am I, striving for spiritual mirth, crossing the barrier of death and birth.

Hearing these loud bellows, the other elder monks hurried over. They disapproved of his initiation as a monk and warned him to be more careful in his monkhood. These monks told the whole story to Lord Mahavir and asked whether this monk would be free from *karma*.

Lord Mahavir replied, "In this very life, this monk will be free from the cycle of life and death."

The Muni ultimately uttained kevalgyana very soon.

The Value of Contentment

There once was a poor Brahman named Kapil. One day his wife asked him to devise a plan in order to come up with some money. He could not think of one, but his wife could. Her plan was for him to go to the king who always donated two grams of gold to that person who came to his palace to wish him good morning. Immediately he got ready to go to the palace at sunrise the next morning. Due to his desire for the gold, he became restless during the night and left his house at midnight to fulfil his desire.

They arrested him and brought him before the king.

On his way to the palace, a policeman interrogated him, "Who are you and what are you doing at this time of night ?"

The Brahman remained silent so they thought that he must be a thief. They arrested him and brought him before the king. Kapil picked up his courage and introduced himself.

"O, King! I am a poor Brahman of your kingdom. I always try to come here to get the gold but when I reach here I am always late. For this reason today, I started my journey at mid-night to receive it."

The King was pleased to hear the truth. He was willing to provide him with as much money as he needed. The Brahman, submitting to the overpowering feeling of greed, wanted to get the whole kingdom from the king.

Then, coming into his senses, he suddenly realised he didn't need money but only mental peace. Therefore, he decided to become a monk and lead a life of self- control and self- discipline.

The Value of Inspiration

Since childhood Prince Prabhava acquired a bad habit of stealing. He owed it to bad company. For many days, he carried out his secret activities but was eventually caught. The king punished him by exiling him from the territory. Having lost contact with his family, he joined a gang of thieves. Endowed with an innate ability in the art of stealing and leadership he became the gang leader of the thieves in a short period of time. As the leader of five-hundred thieves, he now became even more fearless. Even the city guards trembled when they heard his name.

One day Prabhava learned about the dowry of billions of rupees received by Jambu, the son of a rich man on his wedding at Rajgriha. He told his accomplices, "Today we have to go to the wealthy merchant Rishabhadatta's house. There we shall get so much money that if we gave up stealing for the rest of our lives, we would never be in want." As instructed by Prabhava, all the thieves got ready and reached Rishabhadatta's house.

Prabhava made all the servants, gatekeepers and others of the household to pass out into sound sleep through his spell of *"Avasvaapini Vidya."* The yard of the house was filled with riches. The thieves collected it in bundles and broke open all the locks with their lock breaking spells. They were delighted and satisfied with the body.

Prabhava ordered them to leave while they were still safe but to his great bewilderment they could not move an inch from the place. He knew that if they didn't leave, they would all be arrested by the police sooner or later. The moon was about to set and the stars were losing their lustre. The reddish colour of the dawn was visible in the east. He looked in every direction for an escape but he could not find one anywhere. Being puzzled by this, he looked at the upper side from where the light was entering the room through an oriel on the upper story. He climbed up to it and peeped inside to take a look at what was there.

He was amazed to see Jambu, the son of the rich merchant, talking with the eight young wives who were as if the idols of beauty incarnate. Prabhava held his breath

Listening to the talk of detachment in the first night of marriage, he was very surprised.

The Value of Inspiration

and heard the conversation. Listening to the talk of detachment in the first night of marriage, he was very surprised. Jambu Kumar had persuaded his eight wives to get ready for initiation together with him.

In a state of shock, Prabhava thought to himself, "We are both men and how virtuous he is and how degraded I am! He is leaving all his property like dust as if he were totally unattached to it, whereas I am here collecting it and wanting more and more. Prabhava felt himself defeated by the personality of Jambu Kumar.

Appearing before Jambu, Prabhava said, "O Lord! The man who did not bend his head low enough before your royal status is now touching your lotus feet."

Jambu's selflessness left an indelible impression on Prabhava, who also then decided to take initiation. He explained the reality to each of the five-hundred thieves and all of them realized the worthlessness of their deeds. They thought deeply to what Prabhava said and immediately all the five hundred of them got ready to follow their leader and take initiation.

Early in the morning, Jambu apprised his parents and also the parents of his brides of his intention of being initiated. This information made all the parents equally detached. Jambu arrived in the presence of Acharya Sudharma. Acharya Sudharma initiated all the 527 men at a stretch and included them in his fold of monks and nuns.

Later, Acharya Sudharma handed over the responsibilities of his Order to Jambu and nominated Prabhava Swami as his successor. Prabhava, who had not changed himself with the affection of his parents or by the mighty army, being inspired by Jambu's example changed himself and attained omniscience in the lineage of famous *Acharyas* in history.

The Value of Renunciation (1)

Once there was a very poor boy named Sangam who lived in a small village. He faced many hardships in his childhood because of his family's lack of money. One day he looked at a child eating *kheer*. Sangam came to his mother, began to weep and said, "I want to eat *kheer*."

The mother said, "Dear son, how can I afford it? I am hardly able to get even a square meal." Sangam insisted on having *kheer*. He wanted it so badly that he started crying.

The neighbours asked, "Why is your son crying so loudly?" His mother explained to them that he wanted *kheer* but she could not afford it. The lady living next door was very kind and gave her milk, sugar and rice to make *kheer*. The mother prepared *kheer* and called her son to eat it. Sangam, filled with joy, came running to eat it. The mother served the kheer in a dish and told him he could eat as much as he wanted to. She then left for a while to fetch him some water.

As the boy was about to start eating, he saw a monk passing by. Sangam overpowering his own hunger, decided to offer the *kheer* to the monk. Sangam was filled with joy at this idea. He asked the monk to come to his house and receive alms.

The *muni* asked him, "Did you ask your mother or

not?". The child replied, "It is made for me; I have no need to ask my mother. Please accept my kheer in your bowl." As the monk raised his bowl, Sangam poured all the *kheer* in it. He thought he was very lucky, because the great monk would help him achieve emancipation.

The *muni* returned to his place and Sangam's mother came back to the house. She saw her child licking an empty dish. She felt sadness in her heart as she thought how unfortunate she was! He had eaten so much *kheer* and was still hungry. She thought she must be really starving the poor boy.

Sangam did not say anything to his mother about giving all the *kheer* to the monk. After a short while, he felt an acute pain in his stomach. He tried to call out his mother but could not speak a single word. He began to roll on the ground like a fish out of water and soon breathed his last. It was a bolt from the blue for his mother.

He was reborn as Shaalibhadra in the Gobhadra family, the richest family in town, so rich that even the king could not compete with them. He grew up and was married to thirty-two beautiful girls. He never came out of his palace but stayed inside enjoying the company of his thrity-two wives.

One day few jewel rug dealers came to Rajgriha to sell their sixteen rugs. Each rug cost 1.25 *lakhs* of golden coins. They did not find a single person to purchase them, so they went to the king. The king and queen were very keen to buy them, but when the merchants revealed the price, the royal couple was shocked and refused to buy. The merchants were disappointed. They thought that if the king and queen could not buy them, nobody else in the city would be able to buy them. So they got ready to pack up their bags and head for another city when a maidservant noticed their disappointment and inquired: "Why are you all looking so down?" The dealers told their story to the maidservant.

The maidservant laughed and exclaimed, "You have been mistaken. The king is not the wealthiest person in this town. You must go to Shaalibhadra. He has boundless wealth and will be able to buy your rugs easily."

The merchants, relieved by the news, entered Shaalibhadra's abode. They were absolutely mesmerized by the sight of such glory of Shaalibhadra. They were seated in the drawing room. Bhadraa, the mother of Shaalibhadraa was informed and she came to see the merchandise. After looking at the rugs, she remarked, "I need double the number. This is not adequate."

The merchants apologized. Bhadraa, however, ordered her cashiers, "Pay twenty million gold coins to these gentlemen at once." The merchants were impressed by the generosity of Bhadraa. Expressing their gratitude to the maidservant, they went home.

Bhadraa distributed the sixteen rugs among the thirty-two wives of her son, giving half to each. They did not like them but out of respect for their mother-in-law, they used them for one day and then threw them away. The lady-sweeper of the household picked them up, wore one and went to the king's residence. The queen saw her and liked the rug, so she summoned her. The lady told her how she got it and the queen was shocked. She told the king, "We could not buy even one of these rugs to keep, whereas Shaalibhadra bought all of them and then threw them away."

The king could hardly believe his ears. He decided to meet Shaalibhadra. He sent for him through his messenger who met Bhadraa. She replied politely that her son was very delicate. He could not come down even to the first floor of the house. She requested the king to come up himself.

King Shrenik was very astonished by her statement, but went up nevertheless. He waited for Shaalibhadra to come out of his room. When Bhadraa told Shaalibhadra that the king was waiting to see him, he said, "Mother, whatever price is to be paid for purchasing the king. pay it and keep it in our treasure room."

Bhadraa tried to explain to him that the king was not a commodity but he did not understand. At last he was told that the king was their master. He then came out and bowed to the king as instructed. The king blessed him and returned to his palace. Shaalibhadra was perplexed; he could not believe that anyone was superior to him. In order to solve the problem, he decided to meditate and hoped that the answer would come to him. Through meditation, he had a revelation of his previous life and realized that money was not everything. He also started to think about his present weak condition and whether he could ever be satisfied with money. Upon that stroke of wisdom, he decided to renounce his household and his thirty-two wives. After heralding this idea to everyone, he was criticised by his wives, sister and mother.

The Value of Renunciation (1)

Upon that stroke of wisdom, he decided to renounce his household and his thirty-two wives.

They were very aggrieved by this announcement. Shaalibhadra, though adamant in his decision, decided to compromise by forsaking one wife each day instead of all at once.

Subhadraa, Shaalibhadra's sister, was married to Dhanna, a renowned merchant. He was the richest person of his city. When Subhadraa came to know about her brother's renunciation, she became depressed. When Dhanna inquired why, she told him the whole episode.

Dhanna said, "Your brother seems to be a coward. If he wants to renounce the world, why is he delaying it so much by forsaking his wives one by one? He must certainly be a coward."

Subhadraa was shocked at her husband's narrow-minded remark. "How can you say that? It is not an easy thing to relinquish vast property and wealth to lead a life of solitude and simplicity. It is easy to utter mere words, but quite another thing to put them into action", she said defensively.

Dhanna thought about what his wife had said. Dhanna began to feel as Shaalibhadra did and thus decided also to be initiated. He announced, "From now on, I shall lead the life of a recluse and give up my wealth and family, all at once".

Subhadraa could not understand the turn of events. When her husband was prepared to leave, Subhadra a caught his feet and apologized for her mistake. Dhanna, however, replied that he could not go back on his word. He left Subhadraa weeping. He went to Shaalibhadra's house and said, "Come with me and we both shall accept the auspicious path of renunciation." Both left the worldly life to follow the path of Mahavir. They were initiated into the Jain religion and spent their lives in bliss.

The Value of Renunciation (2)

Metaarya was born in a well-to-do and respectable family. Soon after his birth, a goddess, envious of his good looks and fortune, kidnapped him from his family and abandoned him in a forest. A woman belonging to an untouchable caste (Chandal) found him and out of compassion took him home.

In this way, Metaarya was brought as an untouchable. The goddess, who had come to repent her jealousy in banishing Metaarya from the world, tried to atone for her sin by advising him to take the path of renunciation and thereby escape the cycle of birth and death. Metaarya however, was hardly prepared for such a step. He protested that he could not renounce the world without first knowing the delights and temptations he would be resisting.

"My friend," the goddess told him, "it is only possible to rid oneself of something if one is not completely entangled in it."

"But how can I forsake what I haven't had, what I am almost absolutely ignorant of" Metaarya responded. "Renunciation means to give up all luxuries. A poor person's lack of luxuries is not due to spiritual sacrifice but due to economic deprivation. I wish to follow the true path of spiritual good. You may lead me towards it after a set duration. I shall not transgress the time-limit you set."

The goddess was impressed and convinced by

Metaarya's argument. She allotted him twelve years to get acquainted with the pleasures of the world, and helped him to win the hand of King Shrenik's youngest daughter. As the son-in-law of the king, few luxuries were denied Metaarya. Caught up in the enjoyments of being a royalty, he forgot his agreement with the goddess. She, however, was very punctual.

As the time-limit came to its end, the goddess appeared before Metaarya and reminded him of his plan to accept the path of renunciation. Metaarya could not believe or accept what he was being asked to do. So deep was his entrenchment in the allures of materialism that initially he refused to embark upon the path of emancipation as planned. The goddess reproaches and admonitions took their toll and eventually Metaarya succumbed to his duty and became a monk.

Although a monk, Metaarya still dreamed bitterly of the material pleasures he had forfeited. Even during prayers, he regretted the day he had met the goddess. He travelled with the monks from village to village and observed his peers undergoing severe penance, as they busied themselves in meditation and the study of the scriptures (Agamas). In such a spiritual atmosphere, Metaarya could not share with anyone his harsh sense of loss and regret. The restrainful and peaceful life of the monks with whom he lived gave new dimension to his thought. "I lust after the pleasures of the flesh and the material world," he thought, "but these monks are not tainted by any such desire. The peace and serenity that emanate from their faces make me ashamed. Have I strayed from the true path I chose twelve years ago?"

Gradually, Metaarya underwent a complete metamorphosis. He concentrated on his monkhood. Spiritual practice (*sadhana*), adopted under compulsion, became the part and parcel of his life. Engrossed in the life of a monk, he studied the scriptures and adopted a life based upon non-violence as an extension of non-attachment. Many years passed as he performed *sadhana*. Metaarya became lean and thin through long periods of penance. Though physically weak, his spiritual splendour was reflected in his face.

In his journeying through many villages, he once again came upon the town where he had passed the twelve years of opulence. At that time he was finishing a one-month fast. It was the day of his *parana* (the first meal after a fast). In search of alms, Metaarya came to the house of a goldsmith, a man known for his skill and respected by all. On that particular day, he was preparing for King Shrenik a gold necklace made of golden barley grains. When he saw Metaarya, the goldsmith bowed in respect and went into his house to get some offerings. In his absence, a heron sat down and ate the grains, mistaking them for real barley.

The goldsmith returned to offer the alms to Metaarya, then went back to his workseat, only to find the grains stolen. The goldsmith's fear and anger were compounded by the fact that the necklace was being prepared out of expensive material for the king himself. The goldsmith looked about, but found no person there except the *muni*. He questioned Metaarya, who kept silent. Metaarya did not, even by his physical gestures, indicate the guilt of the heron for to do so would amount to killing the bird. A *muni's* vow of non-violence means that he does not commit violence, does not ask others to do it, and in no way supports it, as would the act of revealing the culprit surely do.

The goldsmith concluded, because silence often indicates guilt, that the man before him was not a real *muni* and had stolen the gold grains, and was insolent enough as well to stand before him tauntingly in his refusal to confess and repent. The goldsmith became very angry and abused Metaarya, who kept calm all the while. Infuriated at what he still perceived to be insolence, the goldsmith in his rage brought a long strip of wet leather and tied it very tightly around Metaarya's head. As it began to dry and

Infuriated at what he still perceived to be insolence, the goldsmith in his rage brought a long strip of wet leather and tied it very tightly around Metaarya's head.

compress Metaarya's skull, he still acknowledged no pain and felt no malice or ill-will towards the goldsmith. He was fee from emotions. When the leather dried completely and Muni Metaarya fell dead, he was filled only with peacefulness and so became free from the cycle of birth and death.

Meanwhile, the heron still sitting on a tree and trying to digest its too rich a meal became restless. How, after all, could it possibly be able to digest the gold barleys? The moment that *Muni* Metaarya fell to the ground for the final time, the bird passed excreta and the golden grains dropped to the earth before the goldsmith's shocked eyes.

At first though relieved to have found the precious pieces, the goldsmith soon realized his horrible mistake in killing the man who probably was a muni after all. He then realized that it had not been insolence but serenity that explained the *muni's* silence and tranquillity even in the face of death. He bent down to check if the muni was really dead and at the closer range recognized the man as the former son-in-law of the king.

The goldsmith was now very worried indeed. The first idea to come into his head was to seek the refuge of the *muni:* he bowed down by the side of the *muni* and put on the clothes of the dead *muni.* News of the return and death of Muni Metaarya quickly spread throughout the village and justice was demanded. The people condemned the goldsmith and demanded that he should be punished. Upon hearing the news, King Shrenik was very sorry; he felt as if he had been twice struck in losing both his former son-in-law, a muni, and his best artisan. Nevertheless, he knew he had a duty to fulfil and ordered his soldiers to arrest the goldsmith and bring him before the court.

The goldsmith, in the guise of a *muni,* was presented to the king. Out of respect for the monastic order the king declared that he would not punish the goldsmith in that uniform. He proclaimed, "So long as he is in this dress, he will not be punished; the moment he violates this rule, he will be executed."

The goldsmith had only put on the uniform to escape death, and felt himself far from ready to accept the life of a *muni.* But what else could he do? He joined an order of monks and travelled with them. Eventually he chose for himself the path of detachment and renunciation. Like Metaarya, he became engrossed in meditation, performed penance, and finally attained true liberation.

The Value of Tolerance (1)

King Kanakketu of Shraavasti and his queen Malayasundari had a son and a daughter, named Skandhak and Sunanda respectively. Skandhak was a remarkably intelligent young man. He possessed a great ability to do everything with efficiency. Sunanda's charm and intelligence enhanced her exquisite beauty. Both were extremely fond of each other. At length, however, Sunanda was married to King Purushsingh.

One day a *muni* named Vijaysena came to Shraavasti. Thousands of persons, including Prince Skandhak, came to hear his lectures. After listening intently to the learned monk's profound words, and observing his serene state, Skandhak's ideas about future began to take definite form in his mind. He made up his mind to give up the worldly life and live a truly religious and righteous life. Skandhak confidently approached his parents and told them of his earnest desire to become a monk. As Skandhak was resolute and firm in his purpose, they, at last, gave their consent, and he left to pursue the path of asceticism.

Muni Skandhak, now living among practising monks, began to study the Jain scriptures and perform penance. He engrossed himself thoroughly in his religious duties. Soon he received permission from his guru to lead the life of a recluse.

Thus he began to live in solitude, travelled from village to village and underwent austerities. When

Skandhak's father learned of this, he appointed five hundred soldiers to be the bodyguards of Muni Skandhak. Normally a *saadhak* does not need the help of others. However, due to attachment, Skandhak allowed his father to make such arrangements. As a result, wherever the *muni* went, the soldiers followed.

Despite all efforts, nobody can avoid destiny. Muni at last came to the city of his sister Sunanda. He had completed a month long fast on that day and intended to do parana. The soldiers thought that, because it was his sister's city, there was no need for his protection. Thus they left him unattended.

King Purushsingh and Queen Sunanda were playing chess. Suddenly the queen looked at the monk and

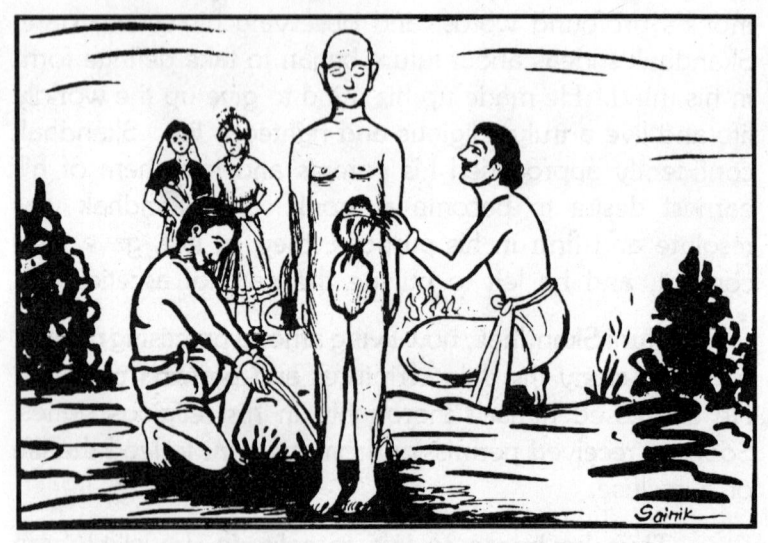

This men then took Skandhak to the crematorium and began to remove his skin.

recognized him as her brother. The king did not recognise the muni, and suspecting the queen, immediately concluded the game and called his henchmen. He ordered them to peel off the skin of the monk. His men then took Shandhak to the crematorium and began to remove his skin. Despite the excruciating pain, the *muni* remained calm.

There were no hostile feelings of enmity or retaliation in the *muni's* mind. He was so intensely engrossed in meditation that he experienced the separation of soul and body. He bore all the tortures very peacefully and attained *kevalgyana.*

The Value of Tolerance (2)

King Bhima of Vidharbha had a beautiful daughter Damayanti whom he nurtured in great comfort and happiness. She married Nala, the son of King Nisadha of Ayodha. When king Nisadha was ready to retire, he transferred the responsibility of the kingdom to Nala, who was a wise and just ruler, with whom the people were happy. However, Nala's younger brother, Kuvara, was extremely jealous of his reputable brother and wanted to bring about his downfall. Knowing Nala's great weakness, his addiction to gambling, Kuvara decided to challenge his brother to a game of dice-- with high stakes.

The brothers usually did not gamble but upon insistence from his brother to make the game more exciting, Nala began younger betting and losing his personal property as well as his towns and villages -- and at last his own ruled city. Kuvara, anxious to claim his spoils before his brother realized he had been cheated, asserted his right to the throne and demanded Nala's exile for twelve years immediately. Nala was hurt and surprised but had no choice. His wife Damayanti - who was not lost as well-- was asked to return to her parent's home. Damayanti, however, as a devoted wife decided to follow her husband. She reasoned, "Would you really like to stay in the forest alone? I want to share the joys and sorrows of your adventures, and do not want to stay behind. Therefore, Nala could not leave his wife behind, though he knew she would face difficulties in the forest.

As they were leaving for the forest, Nala said to his people, "Be as good to my brother as you have been to me. When my period of exile is over, I will return." Nala and Damayanti walked in the forest until evening when they rested under a tree. Looking at his sleeping wife, Nala thought, "I tried to get her to stay at home where she could avoid the difficulties of the forest. I will only jeopardize her safety more if I take her further with me." Thinking this, he left Damayanti in the forest alone and walked on, only to stop, come back, and think "Did we not promise at the time of marriage to share both joys and sorrows together? How can I leave her then?" He pondered some more and then finally left her again after tying a note on the corner of her sari.

Some time later, Nala heard a voice crying, "Nala, come quickly. I am burning. Help me." It was a black cobra in a blaze of fire. When Nala tried to save the snake, it bit him and he was transformed into a hunchback. "This is how you thank me for saving your life?" Nala asked. At that moment the snake turned into a deva, who said, "Don't worry; I am your departed father. Because you have to live twelve years in exile, I've come to help disguise you so that your enemies may not recognize you. Here are two magic things -- a coconut and a basket. If you ever need to change back to your original form, decorate yourself with the ornaments in the coconut and put on the divine cloth in the basket. The deva then pointed in the direction of a city, Sumsumara to which Nala proceeded.

A stray elephant was terrorizing the town, and the king announced a reward for anyone who could bring it under control. The hunchback jumped on the elephant, uttered a mentra called "controller of elephant" and the elephant calmed down to its normal state. The hunchback was taken to the king, who asked the man's identity. "I was the cook of king Nala. When Nala was exiled, I left too and have been wandering ever since." The hunchback was appointed as the head of the kitchen, prepared food for the king, and in no time earned the respect and friendship of the king.

When Damayanti awoke and found her husband gone, she looked all around and then began to cry. She saw a demon standing before her. She became frightened not knowing what to do. She started praying. Few minutes

When Damayanti awoke and found her husband gone, she looked all around and then began to cry. She saw a demon standing before her. She became frightened not knowing what to do.

later when she opened her eyes she found that the demon had disappeared just as he had come. As she raised the border of her sari to wipe her tears, she found the note tied to its corner. She read it and thought, "Perhaps it would be better if I had acted according to his wishes." She recited the *Namaskaar Mantra* and left to find her parent's home. On the way she met the deva who had appeared to Nala. He told her "Your trouble will last for twelve years after which everything will be all right."

After a long journey filled with many hardships, Damayanti at last reached Achalpura where her aunt was a queen. Summoned to the palace, Damayanti introduced herself: " I was in the service of queen Damayanti. When the royal couple was exiled, I left too and have been wandering since." The Queen, not having recognized her, felt sorry for Damayanti and employed her.

Meanwhile, when King Bhima had found out about the exile of Nala and Damayanti (for he'd been away at the time), he was furious. Messengers were sent out to look for them. Finally reached Achalpura where Damayanti was they recognized and brought to her parent's place. However, King Bhima still didn't know where Nala was. A few months later, a merchant who had come from Sumsumara talked of a hunchback who said he had been in the service of king Nala himself. Damayanti heard it and had a messenger sent to the king of Sumsumara with the message that King Bhima was convening an assembly of princess for the second marriage of his daughter. The hunchback arrived by chariot and served Damayanti's family with food cooked by the rays of the sun. Damayanti was now sure that this was Nala because only Nala possessed those two powers - to cook by the rays of the sun and to drive the chariot through the air. She called the hunchback and the two stood face to face, tears in their eyes. After a few minutes Damayanti asked, "Why did you leave me in the forest? Why, even now, won't you reveal your identity?"

With that, Nala put on the clothes and ornaments given to him by his departed father and regained, to everybody's surprise and delight, his normal form. All rejoiced at the reunion of Nala and Damayanti. The twelve years exile period was almost completed and, with the help of king Bhima and the king of Sumsumara, Nala regained his usurped throne and once again ruled over the kingdom of Ayodhya.

The Value of Satisfaction

King Shrenik was sitting in his palace with his queen Chelana. It was a dark night, and the sky was overcast with clouds. Yet bright, intense lightning pervaded the sky. In a brilliant flash of lightning, Queen Chelana was startled to see an old man collecting firewood on the bank of the river. She was greatly distressed by the piteous sight and exclaimed to the king, "O dear, what sort of poor people dwell in your kingdom? Among such poverty, how can your magnificence be justly appreciated?" The king agreed with his queen that something must be done.

The next morning, he summoned the old man and asked him, "Who are you, and why do you take so much trouble in the odd hours of the night?" The man woefully replied, "O king! I am Mamman, the son of a rich person. I have an ox and, with the purpose of obtaining its pair, I labour round the clock."

The king ordered his servant to take the man to the royal stable and to give him the ox of his choosing. Mamman examined the options, but could not select a single ox. He even refused to take those oxen used for the chariot of the king. When the king was informed of this, he asked Mamman, "What type of an ox do you have, that the best of mine won't do?"

"O worthy king," the man dejectedly began, "I beseech you to visit my house, since you are kind enough to wish for my welfare. Please take this slight trouble, and sanctify my dwelling by your presence.

The king consented to go to the house of Mamman. When he arrived, his eyes were dazzled by the brilliance and radiance of an ox decorated with sparkling diamonds. The king then cried, "O fool! The property of my whole kingdom is unable to make such an ox. What a strange person you are indeed! You must surely have an empty belly, and yet you desire to obtain another of this ox, to get a match for this ox? What purpose will they serve you?"

When the king informed the queen about the incident, she too went to see the ox. Having seen everything, the queen exclaimed, "This old man is not poor, but greedy and miserly. None in this world can alleviate a sorrow such as his."

When he arrived, his eyes were dazzled by the brilliance and radiance of an ox decorated with resplendent diamonds.

The Value of Forbearance

Meghakumar was the son of King Shrenik and Queen Dhaarini. One day Bhagawan Mahavir came to Rajgriha. Thousands of people came to listen to his discourses. Prince Meghakumar was tremendously influenced by his lectures. As a result of the great impression left on him by Mahavir's words, he decided to become a monk.

The prince came to Mahavir and said, "O Lord! I have listened eagerly to your lectures, have keen faith in you, and earnestly desire to become a monk." After Mahavir granted him permission to be initiated, Meghakumar returned home and apprised his parents of his wish to renounce the home.

At first they were very reluctant to allow such a thing to happen. Attempting to convince him otherwise, his mother claimed, "You are the apple of my eyes, the heart of my world. How can I live without you? First seek worldly pleasures, then live the austere life of a monk."

Meghakumar pleaded, "Mother! who knows about death? I am alive at present, but I may soon die. Life is momentary. The world is full of sorrow." Thus did Meghakumar finally convince them and obtained their permission to be initiated into monkhood.

After his initiation Bhagawan Mahavir said to him, "Meghakumar! now you are a monk. You must walk, sleep, sit, speak and stand with self restraint.

The first day of his life as a monk passed rather easily. But the first night proved to be an ordeal for him. As it grew dark and all the monks retired for the night, Muni Meghakumar was made to sleep in the doorway. During the course of the night, many monks had to go out and come back. Although they were careful, they could not help but disturb the newly initiated monk (Megha). As a result, he became angry and thought, "when I was a lay follower, all monks took pains to instruct me, but now nobody cares about me. How selfish and inconsiderate they are! Well, I won't stay with them. In the morning, I will report everything to Mahavir."

On the second day, he came to Mahavir. Being an omniscient, Mahavir knew everything about the previous

As soon as, you lifted your leg to scratch it, a hare sat in the vacant place below your lifted foot.

The Value of Forbearance

night. He said to Meghakumar, "where is your patience? Recall your previous life. You were then an elephant. You cleaned an area in a dense forest in order to ward off forest fire. Suddenly once the forest caught fire, all animals gathered at that place. It was so filled with animals that there was no place for putting a single foot down. You had an itching sensation. As soon as you lifted your leg to scratch a hare sat in the vacant place below your lifted foot.

"You wanted to put your foot down but looking at the hare you thought, 'If I put my foot on the ground, this hare will be crushed. It will be an act of sin. Because of your feelings of caring and compassion, you kept on standing for three days. Then the fire wast extinguished and the animals went back to the forest. The hare also left. So at last. seeing the empty place you wanted to put your foot down, but it was too stiff. You fell down and breathed your last. Thus you had shown extra-ordinary tolerance. Now where is your tolerance?"

As Meghakumar went into deep meditation, he attained the *jatis-marengyana*. He recollected his past life, realized his mistake and sought to have better control over his emotions. Now, truly understanding the value of forbearance, Meghakumar again continued in his monkhood.

The Value of Giving Alms

Shreyaansa Kumar, the son of King Somaprabha in Hastinaapur, and the grand-son of Rishabha, seemed to be an exceptional young man. Once he a dream that he watered a grand golden mountain with a jar of nectar. In that same night a rich man named Subuddhi had a dream in which Shreyaansa Kumar made the sun, with its thousands of brilliant rays, shine ever more brightly. Even King Somprabha himself dreamt that a great man was being defeated and he succeeded only with the help of Shreyaansa.

The next day all met and discussed the dreams in the council of the State. Dream readers were called to reveal the meaning of the dreams, but even they could not fully comprehend what such images indicated. Nevertheless, all agreed that Shreyaansa was destined to become something magnificent.

Thus everyone returned contented to their homes. Shreyaansa Kumar, still pondering over his dream, considered what great deeds would be performed by him.

By chance he looked at the highway and he recognized a lean figure approaching him as Bhagawan Rishabha. Because of his purity of thought, Shreyaansa had achieved *Jaatismaran gyan* and realized that Rishabha had been performing penance for the last twelve months. Therefore nobody was offering him food.

The Value of Self-Control

Rishabha had been offered various types of precious jewels, but no one ever offered him food. In return, Rishabha never asked for food. Upon seeing him who had not eaten anything for the last one year, Shreyaansa rushed to meet the Bhagawan.

Shreyaansa implored Rishabha to come to his palace, sanctify it and give him the privilege of becoming a worthy donor. Upon arrival at his home, Shreyaansa Kumar searched for something to offer in alms and found several jars containing the juice of sugarcane, which was traditionally used to end fasts. He offered this juice to Rishabha with great pleasure. At that time Jain *munis* did not use pots to eat and drink but instead used their hands

He offered this juice to Rishabha with great pleasure.

as cups. Thus Rishabha cupped his hands and drank the sweet sugarcane juice.

That was the day of *Akshaya Tritiya*. Now, on that same day each year, many of our Jain followers begin a fast that is observed on alternate days for a full year.

The Value of Humbleness

Once upon a time there was a Guru who had two pupils. Both of them were intelligent and hard working, but one of them was polite, very humble and obedient while the other was rude. Once, on the way to a village, they saw the imprints of a hand and a foot on the soil. The impolite pupil at once spoke: "This is the footprint of an elephant." After thinking deeply the polite pupil said, "This is the footprint of a female elephant and she is blind in one eye. A queen was riding it and she was pregnant." They argued until they reached the village. There the festivities were in progress. The pupils asked someone the cause of the merriments going on there. The villager answered that the king had just gotten a son. Then the polite pupil inquired about the information he had inferred from the prints, and he was pleased to find that his assumptions were all correct.

A few minitues later, both the pupils were sitting on the bank of a river. An old woman came there to fetch water. Considering the pupils to be astrologers she asked them, "My son has been living in a foreign country for twelve years. Please, tell me when he will return." After uttering these painful words, the woman burst into tears and began to tremble with sobs. The pitcher she was carrying on her head fell down. The impolite pupil said to the old woman, "Your son has died and he will not return home." When she heard so, she was deeply grieved. But at the next moment the polite pupil said to her

After uttering these painful words, the woman burst into tears and began to tremble with sobs. The pitcher she was carrying on her head fell down.

"Mother! don't worry, your son has returned home!" Hearing this happy news, she hurried back home and she found her son there. To congratulate the polite pupil, she took him home and extended to him a hearty welcome.

After some days, when both the pupils returned to their teacher, the impolite disciple accused his Guru of partiality. The Guru subsequently tried to understand what circumstances had brought about that accusation. About the first situation the impolite pupil said that he had seen a large footprint on the soil and thought that it was the footprint of an elephant.

When questioned about the print, the polite pupil answered, "There was a little wetness in the sign which is only possible in the footprint of a female elephant, so

I told him that it was clearly the footprint of a female elephant. The leaves of the tree only on one side of the road had been eaten, and so I knew that she was one-eyed. Because only royalty ride on elephants, and the elephant was a female, it must have been a queen who was riding the elephant." Asked about the queen's pregnancy, he replied, "when the queen got down from the elephant, she left imprints of her palm on the ground; since the lines of her palm were vivid on the soil, I thought that she was expecting a child."

The *guru* asked about the second incident. The impolite pupil said that while the old woman was talking with them, her pitcher fell down and so he thought that her son had died.

The polite pupil said, "I saw that the water got mixed with water of the river and the pitcher, made of soil, got mixed in soil. The place was clean, so I knew that the old lady would meet her son."

Having heard the explanations of both the pupils the Guru reprimanded his impolite pupil: "I never taught these things to your colleague. He used his own wisdom which he attained through humbleness and so he was successful in his work. Because of your rude behaviour, you could not develop your wisdom." The impolite pupil bent down his head and stood there feeling ashamed.

The Value of Self-Realization

Dhansanchaya, a rich man of the city of Kausaambi, had a son named Anaathi, who was brought up in a joyful atmosphere and befriended by beautiful young girls.

Though he was born with a silver spoon in his mouth, due to the rise of inauspicious *karmas,* Anaathi often felt acute pain in his eyes, usually followed by pain throughout his body. His parents tried their best to him cure him of his mysterious disease, but all their efforts were in vain.

Being helpless and frustrated Anaathi feared that his ailment might be incurable. He then made a resolution: "If I am relieved of this disease, I vow to become a monk." The next day he experienced no pain in his eyes.

He then made a resolution. "If I am relieved of this disease, I vow to become a monk."

The Value of Self-Realization

Seeing Anaathi free from his illness, all the family members were pleased. He related the story to his parents, got permission to take *Deeksha* and entered the world of monkhood..

Once when Anaathi *muni* was on the way to Rajgriha, he was standing in a meditation posture under a tree. King Shrenik, passing through the town, was surprised to see the handsome young monk and wished to speak with him.

At that time King Shrenik was the follower of Lord Buddha. Shrenik asked Anaathi the reason for renouncing the household. The Muni replied, "I am anaath." King Shrenik assumed that no one had been taking care of the monk. The King offered him all his wealth and promised him to look after him. The king asked the monk to come with him. Shrenik was ready to be Anaathi's Nath.

Anaathi *muni* replied, "You are also *anaath;* how can you be my *naath?*" When the king was surprised at these words the *muni* replied, "Do you think you can buy the authority of becoming my *naath?* I am a monk, I have no need for your wealth."

The *muni* further explained to the king that nobody can be the shelter for others. He got a good impression of Jain religion and accepted it. Anaathi *muni,* after years of performing penance and meditation to destroy his *karmas,* at last attained enlightenment.

This story tells us that there is truly no person or being in this world who is able to give us shelter. We are the makers of our own destiny.

The Value of Repentance (1)

Suvrat was born in a rich family. He had every facility at his home. Although a wide array of sweets were offered to him, Suvrat relished the taste of *kesariya-modaka*. Whenever he desired to eat the *modakas*, he ordered his cooks to prepare the dish and it would be promptly served to him.

One day Acharya Shubhankar with his Order happened to come to the city. Suvrat was so impressed by their serene nature that he renounced the worldly life to become a monk. After his initiation, he studied Jain canonical literature and performed penance.

All other monks praised him for his keen interest in study and penance. The Acharya too was extremely pleased with Suvrat's learning and spiritual practices.

Once the Acharya went to Rajgriha. On that day there was a special function of *modakas*. In each home *modakas* were being prepared. As a result, all the lay-followers were occupied and could not go to receive the Acharya.

A few hours later they came to the Acharya and begged forgiveness for their negligence. The Achaarya asked them how *modakas* prepared. When the lay-followers explained the process of preparing them, the Acharya believed it to be very rich in diet. Thus he advised all the monks not to go to the houses to collect the alms because it would hamper their study and meditation.

The Value of Repentance (1)

All the monks except Suvrat *muni* observed fast on that day. Muni Suvrat remembered the taste of *modakas* which he used to eat as a householder. He did not observe fast and, with the Acharya's permission, went on his rounds for alms.

The *muni* went to every house looking for *modakas,* but was not given any. He rambled on in search of *modakas* from afternoon until evening. The feeling to eat them grew so intense that he could not control his sense organs.

He continued to wander on the roads. It became dark, but all that was irrelevant to him. Like a mad man he was shouting into the night for the *modakas* that obscured all other thoughts.

When a lay-follower named Jinbhadra heard these words, he looked out through his window and was stunned to see a muni in such a state.

When a lay-follower named Jinbhadra heard these words, he looked out through his window and was stunned to see a *muni* in such a state. He understood, that the monk's behaviour was the result of unfulfilled desire for *modakas*.

Jinbhadra came out and requested the monk to come into his house. When the monk started to go in, Jinbhadra asked politely, "Gurudeva, what time is it?"

The *Muni* looked at the sky to determine the hour. He perceived that there were stars and moon in the sky. He could not move a single step forward. "It is already midnight and I am wandering for my food," he replied, repenting deeply.

Jinbhadra implored him to spend the night at his residence. Muni Suvrat, felt ashamed and regret for his action, accepted the advice and stayed there. It dawned upon the *muni* that he should not have done what he had done. He repented over the deed and in doing so he attained the supreme height of knowledge.

The Value of Repentance (2)

Chetak was the ruler of Vaishaali. he had a daughter named Mrigaavati, who married Shataanik of Koshambi. A few years later, she wanted to renounce the world. She put forth her ideas before her family members and they allowed her to be initiated as she wished.

After her initiation, Mrigaavati lived with Sadhvi Chandanbaala who was the head *sadhvi*. Once Sadhvi Mrigaavati and Chandanbaala went to the place of Lord Mahavir. At that very moment, the luminous gods of the sun and the moon in their original forms came to visit Mahavir. After conversing with Mahavir, Chandanbaala went back to the *sadhvi's* dwelling.

Mrigaavati, who stayed on to talk more with Mahavir, soon lost the track of time. When the gods, the sun and the moon returned to their places, it had suddenly become very dark and Mrigaavati ran back to her place. She was rebuked by *Sadhvi* Chandanbaala: "You are a *sadhvi* and thus have no business staying with *sadhus* after sunset." Mrigaavati confessed her lapse and begged forgiveness from her.

That night, after Sadhvi Chandanbaala had fallen asleep, Sadhvi Mrigaavati could not sleep because she was repenting deeply over her fault and soon perceived light everywhere. She had gotten enlightenment (*Kevalgyaan*) due to the atmosphere of purity that surrounded her thinking.

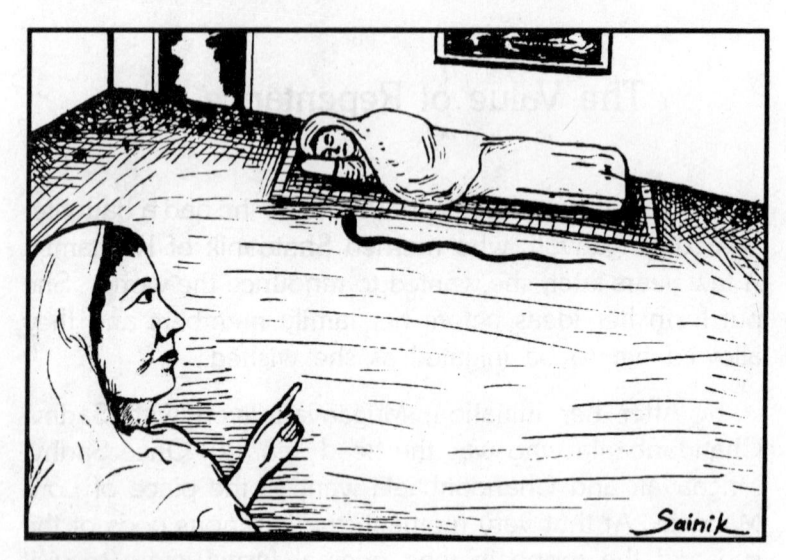

That night, after Sadhvi Chandanbaala had fallen asleep, Sadhvi Mrigaavati could not sleep because she was repenting deeply over her fault and soon perceived light every where.

Since then Mrrigaavati knew everything because she had attained *kevalgyaana*, she saw that a snake was moving by Sadhvi Chandanbaala. She moved Chandanbaala's hand away so that the snake might not bite it. The head *sadhvi* awoke, asked what had happened, and had the story narrated to her by Mrigaavati. Chandanbaala asked how she knew about the snake and Mrigaavati replied she had achieved *kevalgyaana*.

Chandanbaala then thought she had been impetuous in scolding Mrigaavati. She too repented, and thus thinking, felt a flash of light of the supreme knowledge in her and attained salvation.

The Value of Self-Control

The Value of Truthfulness

Anand was one of the most prominent *shraavaks* of Lord Mahaveer. He accepted the twelve vows for a householder. He had twelve million gold coins and forty thousand cows. He used to observe one fast in a fortnight and did *pausadha*.

He observed his vows very carefully and during the last days of his life, he undertook the fast unto death. Due to purity of thoughts he achieved *avadhi-gyana*.

During those days Mahavir came there. Gautama Swami, the chief disciple, went to the village to collect alms.

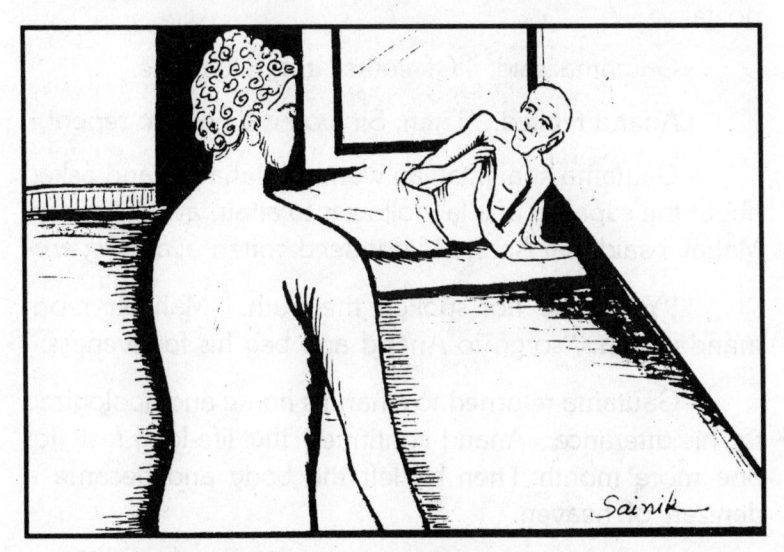

Anand said, "I have achieved Avadhi-gyaana. I have achieved the capacity to know distant things happening in all direction."

When he heard about the *avadhi-gyana* of Anand, he came to see him. Anand paid Gautama the proper respects and asked, "Lord! Is it possible to have *avadhi-gyana* during the lifelong fast?"

"It's not possible in the case of a householder," answered Gautama. Anand said, "I have achieved *avadhi-gyana*. I have achieved the capacity to know distant things happening in all directions."

Hearing this Gautama was awe-struck and said, "A householder cannot have such high capacity to know the objects. You have spoken an untruth, so you have to observe *praayaschitta* for lying."

"Should one who speaks the truth undergo repentance or should the other who tells the lie?" asked Anand politely.

Gautama said, "Of course the latter one."

Anand replied, "Then, Sir, you will have to repent."

Gautama straightaway went to Mahaavir and asked about the capacity of a lay follower to attain *avadhi-gyana*. Mahavir said that Anand had indeed gotten *avadhi-gyana*.

"You have not spoken the truth," Mahavir reprimanded him, "so go to Anand and beg his forgiveness."

Gautama returned to Anand's home and apologized for his utterance. Anand continued the life-long fast for one more month. Then he left the body and became a denizen of heaven.

The Value of Kindness

The Raghu and the Yadu dynasties in India were well-known for their culture and civilization. Since then many Sanskrit poets have been portraying the great leaders of these two dynasties in their poems and stories. Ayodhya was the city which was related to the Raghu Dynasty, and Dwaarika was associated with the Yadu Dynasty.

The history of the Raghu Dynasty has cherished the memory of Rama, an ideal ruler and Sita, his pious queen. In a similar way, the Yadu Dynasty has attained the distinction of producing the 22nd *Tirthanker*, Lord Arishtanemi, and Krishna, Vasudeva and Rajimati.

Two of the most important kings in the Yadu family were Andhakavrishni and Bhojavrishni. Andhakavrishni had ten sons namely Samudravijay, Vasudev and others who were called 'Dashaarha'. Samudravijay's wife Shivaa had two sons named Aristnemi and Rathanemi. Vasudev's wife Devaki had one son by the name of ShreeKrishna.

Aristnemi and Krishna were cousins who spent their childhood together. Being so friendly, they read, played and made plans for future lives together. In games, however, revenge was always in ShreeKrishna's mind as he was often defeated by Aristnemi. Although he was endowed with more energy and physical strength, Shreekrishna could not hurt Aristnemi. In reality, however, they had deep love for each other. When they grew up,

Aristnemi came to be known as the propounder of religion and Shreekrishna, the propounder of ethical code.

Bhojavrishni, another king in the Yadu family, ruled over Mathura. His son, the daughter-in-law, and the grand-daughter were named Ugrasen, Dharini and Rajimati respectively. One of the brothers of Bhojavrishni ruled over Mritikaavti. He had a son and a daughter named Devak and Devaki. The same Devaki was the mother of Shreekrishnna.

Rajimati was stunning and matchless in beauty and behaviour. When she was mature, her parents made efforts to find a suitable match for her. Aristnemi seemed to be fitting the criteria from every perspective except for the fact that he had been harbouring feelings of detachment from the worldly pleasures right from his childhood. He never tried to encumber himself with worldly matters. Ugrasena and his wife Dharini were spell-bound at the handsome personality, virtue and modesty of Aristnemi, but felt discouraged to choose him as a match for Rajimati due to his feelings of detachment.

King Samudravijay and Queen Shivaa, parents of Aristnemi, wanted to get him married as soon as possible but the feeling of detachment checked them to get him married. Whenever they put forth such a proposal, Aristnemi ignored it with a casual smile. One day, King Samudravijay went to Shreekrishna and disclosed his problem. Shreekrishna gladly took on the responsibility and declared that he would not rest till his brother was married.

Shreekrishna discussed the matter with Satyabhaama, a woman of great skill in persuasion and who had the power to impress others by her eloquence. He placed the task in her hands and she also gladly accepted it.

It was a pleasant day of Spring. Satyabhaama got the permission of Krishna to celebrate the Basant Mahotsava (function). She decided to celebrate it on a mountain named Raivatgiri (now popularly known as Girnar). It was a famous hill known for its abundant natural beauty. Shreekrishna, Baldeva and other Yadavas, together with Satyabhaama and her friends reached there as had been planned before. Shreekrishna persuaded Aristnemi to accompany him. All of them were extremely pleased by the atmosphere. Queen Satyabhaama and others surrounded Aristnemi and passed many sarcastic remarks, and made fun of his adolescence. All that appeared very odd to Aristnemi. When the ladies transcended the boundary of respectability and decorum, Aristnemi burst out laughing at them. Satyabhaama, very tactfully and publicly interpreted this laughter as Aristnemi's desire for marriage. Shreekrishna gave this message to Samudravijay, who entrusted Krishna with the responsibility of finding out a suitable match and making all the marriage arrangements.

Satyabhaama proposed the name of her sister Rajimati for Aristnemi. It was, of course, a beneficial proposal. He himself went to Mathura for Rajimati. Ugrasen had already made up his mind for the marriage, so he was pleased at its accomplishment. Both sides made preparations in full swing. On the destined day, i.e., Shravan Shukla Saptami, the marriage party reached Mathura, where King Ugrasen ruled, in the midst of its pomp and splendour.

At that time the Yadavas were addicted to wine and meat. The meal was considered incomplete without these items. They were necessary for the purpose to show off affluence. For this purpose the king had procured many fat animals and birds in cages. They were crying out in terror pitifully and trying to get into the route through which the marriage party was passing.

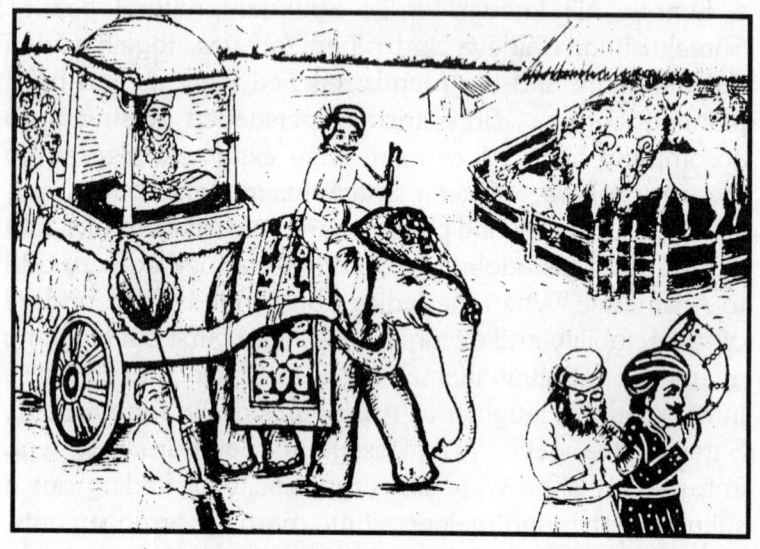

On one side the band of orchestra was creating a delightful atmosphere and on the other side thousands of helpless animals were screaming mournfully.

On one side, the band of orchestra was creating a delightful atmosphere and on the other side thousands of helpless animals were screaming mournfully. Thousands of people passed through the path, but none of them were even moved by the cries of those defenceless animals. As soon as Aristnemi's chariot reached the path, his heart was replete with compassion towards the animals. Puzzled, he asked the charioteer why those animals and birds were screaming and bleating in horror.

The charioteer replied, "O Lord, these animals have been brought here to be slaughtered and provide food during the feast of the marriage party." The heart of Aristnemi revolted against this type of abuse of animals. Suddenly words erupted from his mouth, "Killing of such animals for my sake! It is not for my welfare. What, what, can possibly be the reason for this senseless killing of animals? It is inexcusable and absolutely absurd." He ordered his charioteer to turn the chariot back. The charioteer could not understand what the order was for and looked at Aristnemi. Aristnemi demanded, "Why aren't you moving? Turn back at once."

"But Lord, thousands of people are awaiting your arrival. How can I turn back? The marriage party will be without the bridegroom," said the charioteer politely.

"Whose marriage party? Whose marriage? I refuse to go forth with this nonsense. Take me to Sauriyapur as soon as possible," ordered Aristnemi to the charioteer.

The charioteer, following his orders, turned the chariot back and headed for Sauriyapur. The people of Mathura and the members of the marriage party were puzzled. No one figured out the reason why Aristnemi had changed his mind. Not even a single person was able to decipher the overpowering feelings of nonviolence in Aristnemi's heart.

Shreekrishna, Samudravijay, and Ugrasen rushed to

him to find out the cause. The prince, Aristnemi, said frankly, "Neither side is at fault, but I do not want any animal to be butchered for my sake. I enjoy pleasure and so do all creatures of the world, but to kill them for the mere sake of satisfaction of the tongue is not morally legitimate. Nonetheless, I did not even want to get married but when Satyabhaama and Shreekrishna persuaded me, I really could not refuse. Now, my soul is not ready for it. I would prefer to follow the path of self-restraint and strive to attain liberation."

Rajimati, was considering herself lucky all the time to receive a husband like Aristnemi. It was the happiest day of her life. She dreamed day and night of her bright life of love and happiness. What she did not know was how soon those dreams could dissolve into thin air.

When Rajimati received the news, she was jolted and was knocked to ground senseless, as if her life had just come to an end. Her companions tried to console her and said, "What is the big difference if he has left you? You will get another husband. You need not worry because the actual ceremony has not taken place. As long as the marriage ceremony has not been performed, a woman is not bound to stick to a man. Don't feel nervous. You are learned, tolerant, and our guide too. If a lady like you behaves so foolishly, what will common ladies do?"

Rajimati merged very deep into grief, but when she heard those words from her friends, she awoke and replied, "Is merely going in circles around a fire regarded as the marriage celebration? I was really married from the moment when I decided Aristnemi to be my husband.

From that day I was his and he was mine. All men except Aristnemi are like my fathers and brothers. Aristnemi himself came here with a view to marrying me. The formal celebration is meaningless. It is given importance only by commoners. I attach more value to the union of the heart. That is the reason why I am very anguished at the news of his retreat. These things cannot be explained in words. For he is lucky because he is proceeding on the path of liberation, however, I lament the fact that he did not let me accompany him."

    Finally she made up her mind to give up the household life and be initiated as a nun.

The Value of Calmness

Once a teacher and a disciple, who was yet in his teens, were walking to a village. It was raining and there were puddles of water all around. Suddenly a frog came under the foot of the teacher and died. The disciple drew his teacher's attention to it and asked him if he was going to repent for his deed. Turning a little, the teacher looked at the disciple rather angrily, then proceeded further without a word.

The disciple thought, "I should not have spoken so to the teacher while walking. When the teacher reaches the destination, I should ask him about it politely". However, when the two reached their abode, the disciple bowed down and repeated the same words to his guru. The teacher looked at the disciple with anger and again busied himself with his work.

The disciple thought, "It was not the proper time for such a request. I should have brought it up after the *pratikraman*." However, after the *pratikraman,* when he again asked him about his lapse, the teacher lost his temper and ran after the disciple with a stick in hand, saying, "Stop a bit and I shall tell you how I killed the frog."

When the teacher began to hit him, the disciple ran and hid in a safe place. The teacher, blinded with rage, hardly knew what was going on. Suddenly he collided against a pillar and breathed his last. At that

The Value of Calmness

At that moment his soul, after leaving the body took birth in the form of a highly poisonous serpent known as Chandkaushik, which later on bit Bhagwaan Mahaavir.

moment his soul, after leaving the body took birth in the form of a highly poisonous serpent known as Chandkaushik, which later on bit Bhagawan Mahavir. But the Bhagawan showed immense compassion to it, it achieved enlightenment and repented for all its past misdeeds. Ultimately, after observing lifelong fast calmly it attained rebirth in heaven.

The Value of Controlling Greed.

Merchant Dhanpal of Hastinaapur used to travel to many countries for trade. For one such trip he requested his friends to accompany him. One such friend was Jaichand.

The group started on their way. After a while they stopped under a dense tree to rest there. Jaichand went on to another dense tree to sleep under it. Early next morning, Dhanpal collected his friends and the party set out. All forgot to take Jaichand with them. When he

After a few minutes a drop of honey fell and he licked it.

The Value of Controlling Greed

awoke and found nobody there, he began to walk around. Suddenly he saw an elephant which began to follow him. Frightened, Jaichand ran as fast as he could. At last he caught a big branch of a vast tree, climbed it up and hung there. Since the elephant could not reach him, it tried to uproot the tree.

There was a bee-hive in the tree. Irritated by the motion of the elephant, the bees in it flew about and began to bite Jaichand. Below him was a well with snakes in it and above him were two black and white rats gnawing the branch from which he was hanging. Jaichand was surrounded by difficulties on all sides and death seemed inevitable. At that moment a drop of honey fell from the bee - hive straight into his mouth. He looked at the hive with passion.

A demi-god and a fairy were passing that way and the fairy, who felt pity for Jaichand, forced her husband to save his life. The demi-god said, "He will not accept my proposal because of the greed of honey." The fairy again pleaded with him to do so. The demi-god brought his plane near the tree and asked Jaichand to board it so that they would help him to arrive home safely.

Jaichand said, "All right. Just wait for me until I lick one more drop of honey." After a few minutes a drop of honey fell and he licked it. Again the couple requested him to go with them but he refused and wished to have more drops of honey. Finally the pair was disappointed and flew away. Jaichand wasted his life in the greedy anticipation of more and more drops of honey.

The Value of Self-Analysis

Once upon a time there lived in the town of Rajgriha a thief named Lohakhura. He was a great terror for the citizens. His son, Rohineya, was also a very experienced thief. When Lohakhura felt the approach of his life's end, he summoned his son to him and said, "I am giving you my last advice. Remember it all your life."

Rohineya was very anxious to receive his father's last instructions. Lohakhura told him, "There is a monk named Mahavir in Rajgriha. Do not have any kind of contact with him, you will be led astray from our family traditions. If you chance to pass him preaching to his congregation, do not heed his sermon or even pause to listen."

Rohineya dutifully obeyed his father's last command, and carried on his profession. The magic slippers that could tread upon air and the mysterical science by which one's form could be altered at will, both inherited by Rohineya as family heirlooms, ensured his success and fame as a thief.

One day as Rohineya was robbing a house, the owners returned unexpectedly and immediately noticed something wrong. To avert being caught, Rohineya fled away from the house and in his haste lost his slippers. Running, he came upon a path on which the sanctum-sanctorum of Lord Mahavir was being held. Lord Mahavir was delivering a sermon.

The Value of Self-Analysis

Unable to turn back then, Rohineya had to continue on the path. To avoid hearing the voice of Lord Mahavir, Rohineya blocked his ears with his fingers and ran faster, right onto a thorn. He was caught in a dilemma: if he kept running, he would surely be impeded by the pain and eventually would have to slow if not stop, probably before reaching safety; if he stopped to remove the thorn he would risk both detection and be subjected to the forbidden teachings of Mahavir.

As physical pain overrode all other thoughts, Rohineya paused to remove his finger from his ear and used them to pull the thorn from his foot. At that time Bhagawan Mahavir was dwelling upon the peculiarities of gods. He heard in Mahavir's gentle voice how the gods

As physical pain overrode all other thoughts, Rohineya paused to remove his finger from his ear and used it to pull the thorn from his Foot.

never have twinkle their eyes, they fulfill their work at will, the garlands of their necks never fade, and their legs never touche the ground.

Having disposed of the thorn, Rohineya put his fingers back in his ears and resumed his running. Though he had heard only a small segment of Mahavir's speech and had not listened attentively, he seemed to have retained the words more strongly than he would have desired. The more fervently Rohineya endeavoured to forget the forbidden words, the more firmly they lodged in his mind.

Meanwhile, Rohineya's terror in Rajgriha was increasing day by day. The king's clever minister, Abhayakumar, one day snared Rohineya and tried to extort a confession. Rohineya, however, falsely declared that he was only a businessman from Shaaligraam. Abhayakumar, of course, knew better than to trust a thief, and realizing that it might be easier to reform this criminal than to catch him, he invited Rohineya to dine at his house that evening.

At dinner Rohineya was served food laced with a subtle truth serum. After the meal he become unconscious. He was carried away to a room which appeared like a heaven. There were beautiful women pretending to be goddesses. When, Rohineya regained consciousness, the goddesses asked him, "Oh our dear god! You have become our beloved husband in this heaven. Now, please let us know about your actions in your previous life that were responsible for your birth here. According to our tradition only a dreadful thief can take rebirth here." Instantly came to Ronineya's mind the words he could not escape from hearing in that fateful afternoon, "Gods never have twinkle their eyes......" Rohineya now understood Abhayakumar's method of reasoning in his treatment of a thief, and he began to see the truth behind Lord Mahavir's teachings and the falsity behind his own life. Acknowledging that he was only a human being and not above human laws of morality, Rohineya gained release from his material and immoral bondage. He became a devoted disciple of Lord Mahavir, and to atone for his past sins dedicated the rest of his life to follow a true and righteous way.

The Value of Modesty

After one hundred and sixty years of Veera Nirvana, Bhagawan Mahavira's Emancipation, there was a long famine of twelve years. The Order of the monks was almost disintegrated at that time. The monks hardly got food and milk. Many of the monks even observed lifelong fast as a result. Many others were forgetting their canonical knowledge as a result of hunger and thirst. Bhadrabaahu, who was the successor to Acharya Sambhuutivijay, was the Acharya under whose patronage Muni Sthuulabhadra began his study. Bhadrabaahu and many of his disciples moved to Nepal.

When the famine was over, the monks gathered at Patliputra (Patna) in the state of Bihar where they compiled the first eleven Jain *Agamas*. Bhadrabaahu was the only one who knew the 12th *Agama*, the knowledge of which fifteen hundred monks then asked him to impart to them. Five hundred were to be his pupils and the rest were to be in attendance. Sthuulabhadra was one of the 500 monks. They started the study but soon got tired and quit it but it was Sthuulabhadra alone who studied eight earlier scriptures with determination.

Once when he asked Bhadrabaahu, "How much have I still to study ?" Bhadrabaahu replied, "You have learnt only a drop out of the vast ocean." Muni Sthuulabhadra worked with redoubled energy and learned ten scriptures.

The Value of Modesty

One day when Muni Sthuulabhadra was meditating in a cave, seven of his nun-sisters, having received permission from the guru, came to visit him. When Sthuulabhadra learnt about it, his ego awakened and he decided to impress them. So by using his miraculous power, he turned himself into a lion and waited for his sisters.

When the nuns arrived and found a lion there instead of their brother, they were frightened and thought that the lion might have devoured their brother. They went back to tell Bhadrabaahu, who, having intuition, simply said, "Go back again; you will find your brother." When

When the nuns arrived and found a lion there instead of their brother, they were frightened and thought that the lion might have devoured their brother.

they saw him meditating, they were relieved and paid *vandana* to him.

A short while afterwards, Sthuulabhadra asked Bhadrabaahu to be taught further and was stunned to hear a prompt refusal. Perplexed, Sthuulabhadra inquired, " Why will you not teach me." To this his guru replied, "You are not worthy of receiving knowledge." When Sthuulabhadra probed him further, Bhadrabaahu told Sthuulabhadra to practise self-introspection. On that Sthuulabhadra thought carefully and then remembered how he had egotistically changed his form into that of a lion to impress his sisters. He repented deeply and promised not to repeat such an act in the future.

Bhadrabaahu said solemnly, "Pride is undoubtedly a great hindrance in the acquisition of knowledge."

Only when the whole assembly of monks gathered and implored him, "Please pass on your knowledge of the rest of the scriptures so that we may know them and pass them on in their entirety. Please forgive the lapse of Sthuulabhadra and consider the future of the Jain Order." When requested thus, Bhadrabaahu agreed to impart the knowledge of the remaining scriptures, though without revealing their hidden meaning.

Bhadrabaahu's message was clear: One should not have pride for one's knowledge. Pride leads to destruction. After attaining knowledge, one must know how to use it with modesty.

The Value of Purity

A girl named Bhatta was born to a wealthy family in the city of Avanti. She was beautiful and highly intelligent, but also very stubborn and she unfailingly demanded homage from those around her. When she reached the appropriate age for marriage, Bhatta declared that she would marry a man who would never disobey her, or she would not marry at all.

The condition of Bhatta's marriage spread like fire throughout the city. After the passage of many years without any proposals for Bhatta's hand, Minister Subudhi put forth his proposal to Bhatta's father. The merchant was overjoyed, and Bhatta was at last settled in the domestic life.

Bhatta began her life at her new home. No one, not even her husband, dared to disobey her. Bhatta demanded that her husband should return home every day before sunset, and this command he dutifully carried out until one fateful evening when he was delayed until dark. Being furious, Bhatta locked Subudhi up and did not responsed to his persistent knocking. At last she opened the door, only to run away from the house. She went out and became invisible in the darkness of night.

Alarmed for the safety of a young woman out alone in the middle of the night, Subudhi regretted his wife's brisk stride. As fate would have it, his fears were indeed confirmed. Bhatta was soon abducted by thieves. They wasted little time in stripping her of her valuables and replacing them with a simple peasant garment, then presented her to their leader as a tribute.

Trembling with the rage of insulted pride, Bhatta succeeded in convincing the thieves' leader to keep his distance at least. Tortured daily, she bore the pain in silence but didn't give up chastity.

One day the chief thief's mother remarked on Bhatta's admirable tolerance. She told her son, "She is not an ordinary woman. It will do you no good to torture her. A curse from her lips might bring disaster upon our heads. I advise you, my son, to torture her no more."

As fate would have it, his fears were indeed confirmed. Bhatta was soon abducted by thieves.

The Value of Purity

Heeding his mother's advice, the thief did not torture Bhatta again, but instead sold her to a trader for a considerable sum. The trader, enraged by her refusal to succumb to his immoral advances, started torturing her. Everyday he would take from her body a little bit more of her blood, and with it, her strength, her anger, and her pride.

After some time, Bhatta's brother, in search of his feared but beloved sister, arrived in the city where she was being held captive by the trader. Seeing a girl with the similar features of his sister on the street, he followed her to the trader's house and, explaining that she reminded him of someone, asked the trader about her background and her relation to the trader. Unable to receive a satisfactory reply, the brother specified his questions and recognized the answers as lies. Then being sure that the woman he saw was his sister and that she was not being treated well by that dangerous man, Bhatta's brother offered the trader enough money to get him to confess the truth and sell Bhatta to her brother. Once home, her brother bought Bhatta new clothes and helped her to recuperate. When Subudhi learned of Bhatta's rescue and recovery, he was overjoyed. He brought her back home with all honour.

But this was not the same woman that had stormed into the night not so long ago. Washed of all excesses of emotions such as pride and anger, Bhatta was patient and polite, even gentle, and above all grateful for saving her life from an awful situation among cruel and violent criminals. Her transformation hardly passed unnoticed; news of her respectfulness and inexhaustible virtue reached beyond the household and even beyond the town.

The highest of the immortals spoke well of Bhatta's power of forgiveness and her inner peace. He even proclaimed that no being could compete with Bhatta in this respect. One immortal, jealous of the divine praise accorded to mortal Bhatta, decided to test the woman's virtue. He hid himself in Bhatta's pantry at the moment when two monks came to Bhatta's door to ask for oil for one of the monk's badly burnt hands. Bhatta asked her maid to bring a jar of oil. The invisible immortal pushed the jar from the maid's hands. Calmly, Bhatta requested her maid to fetch another jar. Again the immortal knocked the other container down, and again for the third time the maid was sent for it. Suspecting some superhuman inter, the monks told Bhatta not to worry about it, nor be angry with the maid and they were about to leave.

"I bear malice towards none," Bhatta said quietly. "If you kindly allow me, I shall go myself and bring it for you." As she picked up the vessel, the immortal tried his best to push it from her hands, but all his efforts were fruitless because of the purity of Bhatta's heart. After the monks had gone, the immortal appeared before her and begged forgiveness. He restored the oil in the three containers, so that nothing was actually lost.

The immortal said, "I am overwhelmed by the purity and tranquillity of your soul. I will grant you whatever boon you wish."

"Thank you very much for your kind words," replied Bhatta, "but I am satisfied with all I have. I need no more."

Greatly impressed with her purity, and ashamed of his pride, the god left Bhatta praising and blessing her.

The Value of Celibacy

Rathnemi and Aristnemi were brothers, but the two were poles apart in temperament. Aristnemi was detached whereas Rathnemi was attached to worldly things. The beautiful Rajimati wanted to marry Aristnemi, who refused it being devoted to monkhood. Rathnemi was pleased to learn that his brother had refused Rajimati, for it increased his own chances of marrying her.

So Rathnemi sent his maid secretly to Rajimati to sing his praises. After praising Rathnemi's handsome personality, bravery and skill, the maid put forth his proposal for Rajimati's hand. Rajimati was surprised at that but decided to play a trick in order to teach Rathnemi a lesson. She asked the maid to send Rathnemi personally to get the answer. She added that he should bring his favourite drink with him.

Rathnemi regarded Rajimati's message as a good sign. He went to her house thinking happily about the future. Rajimati greeted him and the two talked for a long time, eventually opening the drink Rathnemi had brought.

Rajimati had the drink with a medicine instantly. Just as Rathnemi was thinking his proposal would be accepted, Rajimati vomited in the same cup what she had drunk from. Rathnemi shivered, wondering if something was mixed in his own drink as well, when Rajimati gave her cup filled with the vomit to Rathnemi and asked him to drink it.

In the same way as this drink was vomited by me, I was abandoned as if vomited by your elder brother.

Rathnemi was startled. Rajimati's behaviour irritated him. He barked angrily, "Rajimati, to ask such a thing is to insult a noble man like me! Do you regard me as a dog or a crow that you think I would drink the vomit.

Rajimati -- I'm just testing your love.

Rathnemi -- Is this the proper way to test it? There are many other methods.

Raji -- If you had just drunk it at my command, I will know that you truly love me. After all, this is the same liquid that you brought for me. I swallowed it but vomited it before it reached my stomach.

Rath-- It makes no difference. After all, it is vomit.

Raji--Why is it so difficult for it to be drunk by the

person who wants to marry me?

Rath--What in the world does marriage has to do with vomiting?

Raji--In the same way as this drink was vomited by me, I was abandoned as if vomited by your elder brother. Rathnemi! When you thought of marrying me, you should have considered that you were really wishing to marry your elder brother's wife. You weren't thinking about anything but beauty. It would've been better for you to renounce worldly pleasures and enjoy inner peace.

Rajimati's words awakened his conscience. He was ashamed. He replied with sorrow: " I apologize for my mistake and will not repeat it in future. I hereby renounce worldly affairs like my brother. Now I shall go."

Soon after, Aristnemi was formally initiated as a monk. Under severe penance Aristnemi attained *kevalgyana* and established a new *tirth*. Rajimati, who had, though not without initial opposition from her parents, remained single, was then initiated into the Order of a nun with her many companions.

After initiation Rajimati wanted to hear a sermon Aristnemi was giving on a mountain named Girnaar. Rajimati in a group of nuns began to ascend the mountain. Suddenly, the sky was overcast with clouds and a severe storm arose. Rajimati became separated from the group and was left wet and shivering.

As the storm calmed and the sky cleared a bit, Rajimati could see a cave ahead. She entered it and attempted to dry her clothes. In the same cave Rathnemi was serving penance. Because of the darkness inside the cave, she could not see him but he could see her. Upon seeing her, Rathnemi could not control his passion and thought how fortunate it would be to get Rajimati in his arms.

When Rajimati realized another person's presence in the cave, she quickly dressed herself and demanded to know who the person was.

"I am Rathnemi who loves you. It is a solitary place and the golden opportunity has arrived. Let us not lose it."

Rajimati, having recognized the voice, was greatly annoyed. She rebuked him, "You are a monk. Your ideals are high. You are serving penance. Why are you talking like a person who is tempted by carnal desires? Think, who you are and who I am."

Rathnemi explained, "Although I am a monk, I am still restless to have you. My only desire is to have you. Penance and spiritual practice lose their importance in your presence, Rajimati."

Raji --You should be firm on your vows. Do you remember your vows?

Rath-- Yes of course I do, but who can see us here?

Raji -- Ask your own soul. Would you not be committing a sin secretly?

Rath-- If you don't want us to do it secretly, we can get married and later on in old age become monk and nun.

Raji--Why didn't you drink that liquid you brought for me?

Rath -- Because it was a vomit.

Raji -- Would you drink your own vomit?

Rath- How can this be? No one drinks a vomit. Why are you talking again and again about vomit?

Raji - You left sensual desires behind when you were initiated and now you want to get them back. Did you put any condition at that time? You are the grandson of Andhakvrishni and the younger brother of Aristnemi. One born in such a noble family would immolate himself rather than accept the vomit. You should stick to your vows and try to keep your ideas pure.

Rathnemi, moved by Rajimati's heartfelt words, realized his mistake and again became engrossed in spiritual practices. Rajimati went to Aristnemi, listened to his sermon, undertook severe austerities and attained emancipation at the end.

The value of Chastity

Jindas was the chief minister of king Jitshatru, who ruled over the town of Basantpur. Jindas and his wife Jattvamalani had a daughter named Subhadra. Their family had a background of deep-rooted Jain traditions. The practice of *Samaayika,* self-study, and chanting of *mantras* was embedded into the routine of their family life. Because Subhadra especially showed much interest and enthusiasm in Jain spiritual practices, Jindas wanted her to be married into a Jain family to avoid any doctrinal conflicts.. However, his search to find a suitable match was at first unsuccessful.

A youth named Buddhadas from Champanagri saw Subhadra on a visit to Basantpur and was so attracted by her beauty and the serenity of her countenance that he collected information about her. He was happy to learn that she was still unmarried. However, then he learned that her father was determined to give her away in marriage to a Jain family. This revelation was a shock to Buddhadas who belonged to a family of Buddhist tradition. He decided to avoid losing neither Subhadra nor his religion through deceit. He disguised himself as a Jain house-holder and performed Jain rituals, i.e., *Samayika,* meditation, religious study, etc. His family was surprised but he was determined to get what he wanted. So, when he felt he was ready, he orchestrated an accidental meeting with Jindas. Finding Buddhadas a capable youth and devout Jain, Jindas gave

Subhadra to him in marriage. But when Buddhadas returned to Champanagari with Subhadra, he threw out his adopted guise of a Jain youth, because its purpose was served.

When Subhadra came to know she had been deceived, she was stunned and hurt, but, because of her inner strength, faced the situation boldly and courageously. As the only Jain in a Buddhist family, she was taunted and ridiculed, but she held her head high and kept her religious resolution.

One day, a Jain monk practising *abhigraha* came to Buddhadas's house to collect alms. Subhadra gave him alms joyfully. When he was leaving, however, she noticed tears falling from his eyes due to a straw stuck in his eye, and knew that monks practising *abhigraha* do not take care of their bodies. Not able to bear the pain in the monk's eye, Subhadra went to him and drew the straw out with her tongue. Her mother-in-law, who witnessed the incident, yelled at her, "You have blemished our home by your indecency! You didn't feel shy of touching the monk? You boast of the Jain religion. Does your religion encourage such activities which are against monastic discipline? Does it not promote lewdness?" The whole family was furious and tried to force her to convert to Buddhism, though she was adamant on her views. Even Buddhadas also expressed doubt on Subhadra's character and started scolding her for the act. Ultimately he stopped speaking to her. She however tolerated everything and indulged in spiritual practices even more.

When the news spread to others in the city, the

situation worsened and Subhadra felt worse. Instead of fearing the blemish on her own name, though, she worried that the Jain religion and its practitioners were being condemned wrongly because of her. Feeling grievous, she once burst into tears, but no one was there to console her. She restrained herself a great deal and kept firm faith in her religion and in her chastity. Subhadra decided to abstain from food and drink until she cleared herself of the false charges, and then absorbed herself in chanting *Namaskaar Mahaamantra*.

On the fourth day of her fast, all four doors of Champanagari got jammed automatically and all efforts to open them were in vain. Because all the roads to go out from the city were blocked, the inhabitants were worried. All of a sudden, a divine voice exclaimed, "Citizens! Your efforts are in vain! Only if a chaste woman, having tied a sieve with a thin thread, draws water from the well, and sprinkles it on the doors, she can open them."

The voice created much discussion and deliberation among the women of the city. Some women appeared to have confidence in their chastity but doubted whether their efforts would open the door. If a door didn't open, a woman was likely to be branded as unchaste. Though most women opted not to participate because of the dilemma, a few picked enough courage, went to the well, tied the sieve with a thread but could not draw any water.

When Subhadra heard of the city's problem and the suggested solution to it, she thought to herself, 'What an excellent opportunity for me to get rid of the blemish wrongly cast upon me'. She said to her mother-in-law, "If

The Value of Chastity

you allow me, I may go and open the door," to which the mother-in-law looked at her with widened eyes and said, "O wretched woman! Do you want a further defamation of our family? Have you forgotten how you acted so immodestly with that monk?" Subhadra was quiet for a moment and then again requested. When her mother-in-law did not answer, Subhadra concluded she was not protesting.

Though people stared at her with suspicious eyes as she approached the well, she paid them no heed and resolutely tied the sieve with a thin thread, mentally recited *Namaskaar Mahamantra* and drew the water, which she took to the doors and sprinkled on three, which

Though people stared at her with suspicious eyes as she approached the well, she paid them no heed and resolutely tied the sieve with a thin threads, mentally recited Namaskaar Mahaamantra and drew the water ....

immediately opened. She left one with the idea that if any other woman would be required to prove her chastity, that door would be for her.

After that event, Subhadra was given a big applause. When Buddhadas and his family knew what happened, they all apologized to Subhadra and felt proud to have her as a member of their household. They adopted the Jain religion. Finally Subhadra became a Jain nun and attained liberation from all worldly bondages.

The Value of Faith

Arnak was a prominent export- import businessman from Champanagari. Though a wealthy man, he also had keen faith in his religion, Jainism. Once a business deal required a massive shipment of merchandise to be sent abroad. Thus he and his business associates set sail.

Suddenly the sky became dark and there was thunder and lightning. Coming rapidly toward the ship, as if in a horror movie, was a terrifying demon with grotesquely elongated features, earrings of real snakes, a blood-covered body and a sword in his right hand. Aranak's ship-mates were panic-striken. They tried to invoke their family gods for help, but to no avail, and screamed, "We're going to die! We'll never see our homes again!" Aranak, however, calmly asked them, "What are you so fearful about? If we're to die now, death would soon be upon us, and if we are to live more no one can make us die. Life and death are but the two ends of life. As such, we should be patient in favourable and unfavourable circumstances alike. Why do we desire to live so long anyway? Why don't we want to die? We shouldn't have fear of death. The gods you worship cannot truely protect you. The true shelters are: 1) Arihant, 2) Siddha, 3) Acharya, and 4) Religion as propounded by the omniscients. Please accept these shelters and you will be free from your sufferings. I myself accept these shelters."

The demon became furious and lifted the ship up in the air and threw it down, causing Arnak's companions to weep pitiously and plead with Arnak to at least say he was giving up his religion, which he did not.

Aranak then declared that he would fast and perform meditation for the remaining trip. However, the next minute the demon approached the ship, challenging Aranak, "Give up your religion and all your companions will be safe; refuse to give it up and I will destroy you all!"

Aranak heard the threat but paid no attention to it, for he was engrossed in *kaayotsarg*. The demon challenged him again and again but Aranak did not reply. The demon became furious and lifted the ship up in the air and threw it down, causing Aranak's companions to weep pitiously and plead with Aranak to at least say he was giving up his religion, which he did not. They complained, "You claim you are a religious person, but you have no compassion in your heart. You will be the cause of death of hundreds of people. How is this compatible with your religion?"

Though both the demon and his companions tried their best, they could not shake Aranak from his faith in true religion. At last, the demon bowed down to Aranak and said that he had heard Aranak was a firm religious person, that no one could divert him from his religion, and had come there to test him. He concluded: "I am very happy to find you steadfast in religion. Please accept a gift of two special earrings and again I commend you on your staunch faith in religion." Other members of the ship echoed similar comments, thanked Aranak, and arrived safely at their destination.

The Value of Detachment

Prince Ardrak of Persia and Prince Abhaya of Rajgriha developed a friendship through the exchange of letters and presents. One day Ardrak decided to meet his friend Abhaya. Ardrak requested his father to let him undertake a journey to Rajgriha. His father refused on the grounds that the journey was too difficult.

Ardrak, however, was restless to go to Rajgriha. He hit upon a plan and leaving his 500 attendants (who were accompanying him on a trip elsewhere) in a jungle, proceeded further alone. At last he reached a town named Laxmipur and became a monk in the heat of intense *vairagya*. As a monk, he continued his ramblings and reached the town of Basantpur. He stood in the posture of *kaayotsarg* in a temple there.

At that time, Dhanshree, the daughter of a rich townsperson, was playing there with her friends. She saw Muni Ardrak engrossed in meditation and mentally decided to make him her husband. Dhanshree returned home and Ardrak went elsewhere.

When Dhanshree was of marriageable age, she said to her father, "I will marry the same monk as I have decided long ago." The father told her, "How can we locate a monk whom we don't know and who is quite unfamiliar with us? How would it be possible for us to give you to him in marriage?"

Dhanshree did not budge an inch from her decision.

When the problem of recognising the muni arose, she simply said, "I will recognise him." Her father made arrangements to find him and Dhanshree began distributing alms to monks and nuns daily. Finally, when Muni Ardrak reached there, Dhanshree recognised him and informed her father, who soon came there and pleaded to the monk, "O holy monk! The life of my daughter depends upon you. Please accept her as your bride or else she will languish to death. You will be held responsible for the death of a girl and for this you may run into difficulties."

The innocent *muni* got entangled in the net of her father's wishes agreed marriage. Ardrak and Dhanshree were married amidst great pomp and show and began to live together thereafter.

Ardrak saw that his son had encircled his body with the thread twelve times.

After some years, Dhanshree gave birth to a son. When the son grew up, Ardrak again decided to renounce the household. When Dhanshree knew his intention, she became sad but knew Ardrak was firm in his decision. Seeing his mother's tearful eye, her son asked her, "Why are you weeping?" Dhanshree replied, "Your father is leaving both of us to live the life of a monk."

The son said, "How can my father go? I shall tie him so that he cannot go away." The son got up and tied his father with cotton thread.

Ardrak saw that his son had encircled his body with the thread twelve times. He was greatly moved by the affection of his son and decided to remain a householder for twelve more years.

Completing the twelve years, he got himself initiated with his wife's permission and once again left for the Rajgriha. When he arrived there, Prince Abhayakumar was wonderstruck to learn of his friend's adventures. Muni Ardrak stayed there for a short period and then went to Lord Mahavir. In the concluding phase of his life, Ardrak attained emancipation through deep meditation and penance.

The Value of Patience

The great lady Anjana was the daughter of Queen Hridaysundari and King Mahendra. Because she was the only sister of a hundred brothers, her parents and all her brothers loved her very much. Sweet and charming, she impressed everyone at first sight. Because of her extraordinary beauty and talent, it was not easy to choose a groom perfectly suited to her.

The King's chief minister, whose help the king sought in the matter, had two princes in mind: Vidyutprabha, the son of King Hiranyabha, and Pavananjaya, the son of King Prahlada. The astrological readings of the two, however, were that the former would die at eighteen whilst the latter would have a long life. After some time, King Prahlada sent a marriage proposal to King Mahendra, who accepted it. All agreed to a date for the wedding ceremony.

A week before the ceremony was to take place, Pavananjaya convinced his friend Prahasit to come with him to glimpse Anjana before the marriage. They surreptitiously entered into Anjana's room, hid themselves when they saw a group of women and listened to the ongoing conversation.

One of Anjana's many friends praised Pavananjya, while another praised Vidyutprabha. Then Anjana said, "You know, Vidyutprabha is lucky that he has left carnal desires and will attain liberation very soon". Pavananjaya, thinking that Anjana loved Vidyutprabha, at first wanted to leave the town but then decided to divorce Anjana after the marriage.

After the marriage Anjana waited in her room for her new groom, who did not show up. Pavananjaya did not acknowledge her as his wife. Anjana, not knowing what wrong she had done suspected the force of her previous life's karma at work and knew she must just wait it out.

After twelve years had passed without any communication between the two, King Raavan sent King Prahlada a message that in order to defeat King Varun he would need his help. King Prahlada prepared himself to lead the army, when Pavananjaya offered himself to go, a proposal to which the king agreed. Thousands of people gathered at the city gate to see the prince off, shouting blessings and good wishes. When he saw Anjana in one corner of the crowd, he became upset, muttering under his breath, 'What! Is she still trying to attract me? She never loved me, but only him. She has no right to take away my moment of fame by being here."

That night when the army was a few cities away and resting, Pavananjaya was watching a pair of skylarks enjoying each other's company. After a while the male flew away, leaving the female to burn in the agony of separation. The emotions of those birds left a deep impression on Pavananjaya, who thought, "How distressed the female skylark is when her partner has left her! How deep must be Anjana's distress! -- She has been living a life of neglect and unhappiness for twelve long years, and I have been responsible for her misfortune!"

He conveyed his feelings to his friend Prahasit, who

The Value of Patience

replied solemnly, "I cannot measure the depth of Princess Anjana's wound. She is noble, patient, and forgiving. You think you have given her up, but you do not realize how devoted she is to you. Do not doubt her chastity of mind and heart."

The friends decided to use the divine power they had to fly to Anjana's palace. Anjana was surprised and glad to see her husband, whom she first mistook for a ghost or god. The night was warm and the two made up for the lost time. Before he left in the morning, he gave his wife a ring with his name inscribed on it as proof of his spending the night in her room.

Soon after Anjana found out that she was pregnant.

As physical pain overrode all other thoughts, Rohineya paured to remove his finger from his ear and used then to pull the thorn from his Foot.

When her mother-in-law knew, she called Anjana a slut and informed the king, who agreed to have Anjana dropped off in some dense forest near her parents' home.

If she had not been so sad, Anjana might have found the situation ironic. She had patiently suffered the misery of twelve long years of neglect by her husband, and then a one night's meeting with him had so much more disastrous consequences.

Anjana, on her friend Basanttilka's insistence, went to her parents' house, where she did not receive a welcome any better than the one she would have received from her husband's household. Her parents, brothers and sisters-in-law, hearing of her supposed predicament called her loose charactered and ostracized her just the same as everyone else. So Anjana and her friend went away to take shelter in the forest.

Anjana gave birth to her son 'Hanuman' in a cave in the forest. Anjana's maternal uncle, Pratisurya, saw the ladies from the air and thought they must be in need of help. He took them to his city, where both Anjana and her son where respected.

Meanwhile, Pavananjaya came back after twelve months, becoming victorious over Varuna. Though he was welcomed by all the citizens of his kingdom, when he inquired of people about Anjana, he came to know that something was wrong by the looks on their faces. When he heard the word 'exile' a pang of sorrow overtook him and the joy of the victory faded away. He rushed to his in-laws house where the news was the same.

He decided to find Anjana or die. He resolved not to eat anything until he met his loyal wife once again. Envoys were sent in all directions and Anjana was found in the city of 'Hanupur' and was brought back to Pavananjaya's city. Her parents and parents-in-law, upon hearing the truth, shed tears of shame and regret for having judged her too quickly. Anjana consoled them all by saying that her misfortune was the outcome of her own *karma,* they were merely instrumental.

After Pavananjaya had ruled over his father's city for many years, he renounced the world to devote the remainder of his life to spiritual attainments. The ever-patient Anjana practised severe penance, took a life-long fast and was reborn as a celestial being.

The Value of Monkhood

A little boy named Thaavaacha Putta was standing atop his home and enjoying the natural beauty of the landscape when a sweet melody from a neighbouring house reached his ears. Curious of its nature, he went to his mother and asked her what it was and what was its significance. His mother told him that the songs were a part of a celebration to welcome a newborn child.

"Were such songs sung at my birth also?" Thaavaacha Putta asked.

"Yes, my dear," his mother answered. "Songs more in number and sweeter than these too."

"Mother, I feel almost as if I have never stopped hearing them."

"Go and listen to them then, my son."

Thaavaacha Putta went back to the roof and listened to the singing. The songs, however, were not as pleasant then. They were harsh and shrill and filled him with a sense of uneasiness. Again he ran to his mother and asked, "What has happened to the songs, Mother? Why are they no longer sweet but strident? Are they being sung by some other person?"

"No, son, the same person is singing, but--"

"Why, then, are they different than before?"

"The circumstances have changed," she answered.

"The child who was born a few hours ago has died. That is why the songs have changed into mourning songs."

The child who was born a few hours ago has died.

Thaavaacha Putta was badly shaken by the incident. Full of sorrow, he asked, "Why do people die? Does it not matter how small the person may be?"

"Now don't ask such questions," said his mother rather irritatibly.

"But mother," he protested, "tell me one thing. Will I too have to die in this manner?"

"Not only you, but also I, your father, and everyone will have to die some day, and will be born again according to the good and bad deeds they have done."

Somewhat confounded, Thaav-aacha Putta asked his mother, "Is there any way to escape the cycle of birth and death?"

"There is," his mother admitted, "but it is a very difficult and severe course of life. The only path to spiritual liberation is to perform *Sadhana* at the feet of Lord Aristnemi, the 22nd *Tirthankar* of the Jain tradition. But it is a life-long process, my son."

"Mother, where does Lord Aristnemi live now? Will he come to our village soon?"

"Yes, he will, my son, and if you wish you may meet him then."

Thaavaacha Putta had decided to adopt the life of renunciation and penance to liberate his soul and so escape the cycle of life and death. From that day on, a detachment toward worldly things filled his mind and occupied his soul. When Lord Aristnemi came to his town, he was initiated into the monastic Order and ultimately proceeded on the path to enlightment and emancipation.

The Value of Self-Awareness

It was just before midnight and Kamdeva, a follower of Bhagawan Mahavira was deeply immersed in his meditation. Suddenly he was confronted with a horrid and demoniac figure.

"Kamdeva, give up practising your meditation and your moral values or else I will decapitate you with my powerful sword" ordered the demon in a derogatory voice. Kamdeva, however, was in a state of higher self-awareness and deep meditation and felt no fear. Mentally he was completely unperturbed.

"Kamdeva, give up practising your meditation and moral values or else I will decapitate you with my powerful sword" ordered the demon in a derogatory voice.

When the demon noticed this, he became annoyed and enraged at the same time. He decided to make another approach and assumed the shape of a giant elephant. He hurled himself towards Kamdeva and threw him up into the air with a powerful force. When Kamdeva landed, he trampled his feet on him. To the demon's dismay, however, Kamdeva was still completely unaffected and his meditation went on undisturbed.

At this point, the demon was absolutely furious and could not believe his eyes. As his last resort, he adopted the form of a fierce serpent and repeatedly stung Kamdeva with his poisonous venom. Still Kamdeva remained in complete tranquillity. The demon accepted his defeat and left after an apology.

One day it happened that Lord Mahavir came to the town.

Lord Mahavir called many monks and nuns and announced the news: "Worthy monks, Kamdeva is a householder, but yet he has attained a remarkable degree of self-awareness. He has stoically endured all the tests he was put to by the divine powers. He has achieved the *summum bonum* of life. Being monks, your self-realization, equanimity, stoicism, and concentration should be of an even higher level." Self-awareness is an eternal burning lamp that lights many more lamps.

GLOSSARY OF TERMS

Abhigraha : Self-imposed restriction in the matter of food, etc.

Acharya: Head of a Jain order

Aagmas: Holy scriptures of the Jain religion; Jain canonical texts; 32 in number

Akshaya Tritiya: A Jain festival celebrated on the day the first Tirthankar, Rishabha, did parana after having observed a one year fast.

Alms : Food given by laypersons to monks and nuns

Anaatha : Any person who is without a lord (or a protector)

Arihant : Jin; literally conqueror of inner enemies, i.e., passion, hatred, greed, attachment, etc.

Avadhi-gyana: Extra-sensory perception or clairvoyance

Avasvaapini Vidya: Science of making others fall asleep; a type of hypnosis

Brahmin : A person who is born in the uppermost of the four castes in the Vedic society; they perform religious and householder's rites and rituals

Chakreshavari : Attending deity of the Tirthankars; since the Tirthankars are free from attachment, it is not they that help devotee, but rather the attending deity

Chandaal: An 'untouchable' person

Chaturmaas: Four months of rainy season; period in which Jain monks and nuns are not allowed to go from one village to another, but rather spend their time in one place

Deeksha: The formal process of initiation into monkhood or nunhood; the vows one takes to become a monk or nun

Deva : A god

Fast: Ritual of not eating or drinking for 36 hours (2 nights, 1 day), except water during the day

Jaati Smaran: Memory of previous (past) birth(s)

Jinakalpa: The Practise of a special code of conduct by the Jain monks resembling a jina or Tirthankara

Kaayotsarg: A standing posture of meditation peculiar to Jain religious practitioners; literally 'giving up attachment to the body'

Karma: The subtle material particles attracted by the activity of the soul; elimination of karma particles, good and bad, is necessary for the liberation of the soul

Kesariya-modak: A sweet prepared from wheat flour, sugar and clarified butter called ghee, with saffron added for colour and flavour

Kevalgyaana: The supreme state of knowledge attained through penance and meditation and after the attainment of which one is emancipated from the cycle of birth and death

Kheer: A special dish prepared from milk, rice and sugar with raisins etc. added

Lakh: Term meaning one hundred thousand

Lord Aristnemi: The 23rd Tirthankar of the Jain order

Lord Mahaveer: The 24th or the last Tirthankar of the Jain order

Mahaapraana: A kind of meditation to exert control over the vital force.

Mantra : Holy canonical text, a syllable to be chanted internally or vocally; prayer

Muni : Monk; one who has left the home for spiritual practice

Naath : Owner; lord, protector

Namaskaar Mahaamantra: Sacred Jain mantra paying obeisance to Arhats, Siddhas, Acharyas, Upaadhyaayas (teachers), and all monks and nuns. Navakaar Mantra, Nommokaar Mantra and Namaskaar Mantra are all synonymous with the term

Paaranaa: First meal taken after observing fast

Paatri : A pot a bowl made of wood; Jain monks and nuns use it for food water, etc.

Pausadha: A kind of Jain spiritual practice in which a householder observes a fast and other Jain religious rituals

Praayaschitta: Repentance performed before a guru for one's mistake

Pratikraman : A kind of self-introspection which is to be done daily by Jain monks and nuns and by lay followers fortnightly or yearly

Rupees: Indian currency

Saadhaka : Spiritual practitioner

Sadhvi : Nun

Samaayik : A 48-minute period of concentration for the attainment of equanimity, for the abandonment of all sinful acts or thoughts

Samavasaran: A place where Lord Mahavir delivered lectures

Santhaaraa: Life-long fast (fast unto death)

Shraavak/shraavikaa: Lay followers of the Jain order, both male and female, observe 12 vows prescribed as a code of conduct for Jain householders

Siddha : A liberated soul who has overcome the passions and is complately free from the bondage of karma

Tapasya: Fast for a period longer than the usual 36 hour fast

Tirth: Order, which is four-fold, consisting of monks, nuns and lay followers

Vairagya: Detachment

Vandanaa : A gesture by lay followers to pay homage to Jain monks and nuns. It is done sitting on the toes with the knees on the ground, putting the palms together, and bowing down.

RECOMMENDED READING

The Art of Positive Thinking
—a book by Acharya Shri Mahaprajna

ISBN: 978-81-319-0166-3
Size: 6"X9.25" | PB | Page: 236

The book is devoted to a detailed discussion of the following three topics:
- The art of thinking
- Principles governing the change of heart
- Freedom from fear

The Art of Thinking
Man is a living being endowed with a mind, and thinking is a function of the mind. The body and the mind are intimately connected to each other. The body influences the mind, but the mind affects the body much more. Constructive thinking helps in better relationships and progress in mans life. So, the practice of *preksha dhyana* wipes out negative thinking and promotes positive thinking.

Change of Heart
The evolution of our world is for change. A complete change of heart takes place by the internal transformation, which is threefold – transformation of emotions; thought; and body.

Freedom from Fear
There are five main sources of fear and their five main reactions.

B. JAIN PUBLISHERS (P) LTD.
1921/10, Chuna Mandi, Paharganj, New Delhi-110055 (India)
T: +91-11-4567 1000 | F: +91-11-4567 1010 | E: info@bjain.com | W: www.bjain.com

RECOMMENDED READING

The ART OF POSITIVE THINKING

ACHARYA SHRI MAHAPRAJNA

The true greatness lies in being kind,
The true wisdom in a happy mind.........

ISBN: 978-81-319-0166-3
Size: 6"X9.25" | PB | Page: 236

A thought provoking book on the daily discourse by Acharya Shri Mahaprajna at the Shivirs that took the shape of the book- 'Kaise Sochen' in Hindi. It is a meticulous endeavour by the author that leaves a deep impression on the reader's mind.

The Art of thinking; the techniques of bringing about a transmutation in the mind is discussed in length. It is an important means of achieving freedom from fears like that of disease, old age, death, forgetfulness and madness.

- Helps to wipe out negative emotions, promotes positive thinking
- Leads to full self-realization
- Interesting lucid presentation
- Inclusion of short-stories, anecdotes, and self experiences with scientific and logical explanation
- Each chapter leaves the reader with a thought to ponder over

B. JAIN PUBLISHERS (P) LTD.
1921/10, Chuna Mandi, Paharganj, New Delhi-110055 (India)
T: +91-11-4567 1000 | F: +91-11-4567 1010 | E: info@bjain.com | W: www.bjain.com